DISCOVERING THE SUPERNATURAL

Interacting with the
Angelic and Heavenly
Realms in Your Daily Life

DOUG ADDISON

D1361976

For ordering information contact:
InLight Connection (800) 507-7853
PO Box 7049, Santa Maria, CA 93456
DougAddison.com

Cover Design by Christian Wetzel

Book design by Treasure Image & Publishing
TreasureImagePublishing.com (248) 403-8046

CONTENTS

ACKNOWLEDGMENTS

I would like to thank my wife Linda for her endless support and love for me and all of the long hours spent with God in preparing for and writing this book.

I extend a special thank you to those who make all of this possible—the InLight Connection Writing and Publishing Team—Krista Abbott, Beverly Simons, Arlene Brown, Dee Collins, Shannon Crowley, Caitlin Nightingale, and Joel Maust. Your tireless work and dedication to this project is greatly appreciated.

Thank you to Christian Wetzel for sharing his graphic art talents with us in designing the book cover, to Jenny Collins for her creative direction on titling, and to Sherry Ward of SquareTree Publishing for her *eagle eye* for final proofing.

ENDORSEMENTS

Doug Addison is a tremendous communicator of deep spiritual truths and activations. His book, *Discovering the Supernatural*, will bless the "hungry reader" and take you on a journey of revelatory discovery and supernatural encounter.

Patricia King
Founder Patricia King Ministries

Discovering the Supernatural is an exciting reminder of God's desire to bless and use His children. You and I have been given the wonderful opportunity to partner with Jesus on a daily basis, and that includes partnering with Him in supernatural ways. If you hunger to bring Heaven to Earth through the beauty and power of the gifts of the Holy Spirit, this book is a must read.

Through faith-building scriptural insights and practical wisdom, Doug points to the grace of the Cross. As you read the pages ahead, you will be freshly inspired to press into everything that has lovingly been made available to you and ultimately touch those around you with Christ's irresistible love.

Georgian Banov
President and Co-Founder of Global Celebration and the Global Celebration Schools of Supernatural Ministry in Harrisburg, PA, and New York, NY

Discovering the Supernatural is like being handed a road map to exploring the subject that offers both firm theological teaching but also hands you faith from the author himself.

Doug has applied his rich journey to define a safe and broad context into the supernatural and to encounter God the way He has always longed to be encountered by humanity. I read it, I love it, and I recommend it.

Shawn Bolz
TV Personality
Author of *Translating God,*
God Secrets, & *Growing Up with God*

I love Doug's new book. The revelation on interacting with the angelic and heavenly realm is quite awesome—but not so much so that you would disqualify yourself from that ever being something you could step into.

I particularly love how practical, understandable and full of wisdom this book is. For anyone drawn to experience more of the heavenly realm this is as good a tutorial as there is.

Johnny Enlow
Author of *The Seven Mountain Prophecy*

Have you ever said, "There has to be more to experience in life as a Christian?" Doug Addison has discovered the way to get the most out of your salvation experience.

Discovering the Supernatural: Interacting with the Angelic and Heavenly Realms in Your Daily Life will give you the keys that are necessary to unlock the Revelation 4 door that calls you heavenward to tap into the spiritual inheritance we have received as joint heirs with Christ.

When you apply these biblically based doctrines to your spiritual disciplines your life will take on an exciting new expression of Jesus Christ.

Dr. Barbie L. Breathitt
Prophetic Dream Life Coach "Ask Barbie"
Author of the *A to Z Dream Symbology Dictionary*

Doug Addison is a long-time friend of mine and I trust the prophetic words and insights he receives through supernatural encounters.

I am very excited about Doug's book, *Discovering the Supernatural,* which gives an eye opening account of some of the heavenly encounters he has personally experienced.

In this book Doug not only shares his personal experiences, but he demonstrates how you can open the heavens over your own life in a way that will activate the supernatural, cause angels to move on your behalf, and help you access and operate in the Courts of Heaven.

Joan Hunter
Author and International Evangelist
President Joan Hunter Ministries

Doug goes deep and reveals hidden secrets of the supernatural that he normally only reserves for one on one mentoring. If you've always wished you had a mentor that could answer all your deep questions on how to connect to God, the supernatural, angels, and set yourself up for visitations from Heaven, God has answered your prayer!

This may very well be Doug's masterpiece of all his books as he takes a risk to open up to you the realms of the supernatural and open heavens like never before released to the public in this way!

Fasten your seat belt as you are about to embark on a journey beyond the stars into the very throne room of God as you *Discover the Supernatural.*

Dr. David Herzog
Author and International Evangelist
Founder of *The Glory Zone*

Once I picked up this book, I couldn't put it down. The best thing about it is—it makes everything about the supernatural ways that God communicates, completely accessible and understandable!

Doug Addison skillfully unpacks the supernatural in such a simple way. This book is easy to read, yet at the same time has such depth of revelation, you will come into a new understanding of God and His ways.

Your life is about to change in the best way possible because suddenly understanding how to discover the ways of God, will become plain to you.

Elizabeth A. Nixon, Esq.
Author of *Inspired by The Psalms—Decrees that Renew Your Heart and Mind*

Doug Addison is the best person I know to write a book on *Discovering the Supernatural* because he walks in heavenly encounters all the time. His vast experience in these areas have equipped him to help others to walk in the same encounters he has.

If you are hungering for more of the supernatural in your life, then read this book. Then get ready to be pulled out of the bondage of your past and into the new season God has for you!

Katie Souza
Author & International Evangelist
Founder of Expected End Ministries

PREFACE

For those of you who do not know me, I place a very high value on helping people hear God for themselves. This includes studying the supernatural encounters that He initiates.

I believe it is important to value these encounters by recording and studying them. By doing this, we get to know God better through the ways He communicates with us—from the big dramatic ways to the quieter, more personal ways. All of these are good ways to hear Him!

For many years now, I have been teaching people how to hear the voice of God, understand their dreams, and (my specialty) find their destiny.

I am a prophetic speaker, author, and life coach. I have a blog and podcast that I update weekly; I am also an experienced dream interpreter and spiritual life trainer.

I have traveled all over the world bringing a message of hope, love and having fun. These things have expanded my perspective and experience with God, giving me insight into ways to help others hear God better, too.

That being said, I do consider this book to be a ministry school–level training for you. I normally do not teach this material outside of ministry schools because it does require a certain level of maturity. But I felt like God told me to go ahead and write this book for people who are ready to go deeper with God and experience the supernatural in their daily lives.

Blessings,
Doug Addison

PART ONE

ENCOUNTERING THE SUPERNATURAL

CHAPTER 1

INTRODUCTION

The way you and I were taught to hear God and understand the supernatural realm is pretty different from what I will talk about in this book. My goal is to help you *learn to discern*. I want this book to feel like a place you can learn and grow, while helping you feel comfortable enough with the supernatural to ask yourself questions along the way.

Some of the specific things I cover will address questions I had along my journey or questions others have asked me as they have learned to hear God and understand the supernatural.

I share a lot of stories about ways God has spoken to me, and supernatural experiences I have had, to help you learn from real-life examples. After all, that is one of the best ways to learn!

Not to mention, there are so many stories throughout the Bible where radical, supernatural things happened. We just need to have the *eyes to see* and the *heart to understand* what God is doing. I will also discuss many of the encounters in those Bible stories you grew up reading.

What We Will Cover

The day I started this project, I got really excited because God woke me up and gave me some more revelation and direction for this book.

We are going to talk about opening the heavens over your life, as well as recognizing and activating angels. You will probably have a lot of questions! So, I have included some questions others have asked me at different times and the answers I provided.

Here are some other areas I am going to cover:

- How to open the heavens over yourself
- Living out prophetic words
- Switching from seeing demons to seeing angels
- Supernatural encounters in the Bible
- How to discern the counterfeit versus the real

I cannot emphasize this enough: discernment is very important when we are dealing with the supernatural. So, I will go through learning to grow in spiritual discernment—having the *eyes to see.*

I will also talk about the Courtroom of Heaven. I go there a lot, actually. In 2013, I had a visitation from Jesus that I will share with you. It is a pretty wild story. I hope you are ready!

Finally, we will end with an activation prayer to open your spiritual eyes.

No matter how much training you have had, I want you to know that you are welcome here and I am excited you are diving into this book. No matter where you find yourself in your spiritual journey, I am very glad that you have chosen to learn more.

I normally teach this material in supernatural schools around the country. In addition to my own online ministry school, I have taught for *Bethel School of Supernatural Ministry*, and Randy Clark's *Global Awakening School of the Supernatural.*

I have trained people all over the world, but until now, I have never pulled this material together in order to release it to everyone.

PREPARING FOR THE SUPERNATURAL

Why Teach on Supernatural Encounters?

Today, many people limit God by their own beliefs and experiences, and especially their own understanding. I think many people are comfortable experiencing God through reading their Bible or going to a worship service. But God is way bigger than church services or just reading your Bible. So fasten your seat belt!

Most people are comfortable with the healing miracles they read about Jesus performing in the Bible. But when I read the Bible, my eyes and heart are open to experiencing God for myself, and I experience supernatural encounters that are strange sometimes. I want to share those with you and activate this in your life as well.

I will answer some questions along the way, and then I will pray for you. I am going to share some deep things that you will not learn on a typical Sunday morning. You are going to have some experiences yourself and I am confident that you will encounter God.

Noticing the Unexplainable

By now you may have noticed that there are some things in the Bible that you cannot really explain. Think about it: the Red Sea parts (Exodus 14), donkeys talk (Numbers 22:21–39), and even thunder speaks (John 12:27–29), and water turns to wine (John 2:1–11). An angel performs a prison break (Acts 12:5–17), and in another incident, prison doors are thrown open by an earthquake (Acts 16:16–40)!

Another time, Jesus divinely disappeared into an angry mob that was trying to kill Him:

"All the people in the synagogue were furious when they heard this. They got up, drove him out of the town, and took him to the brow of the hill on which the town was built, in order to throw him off the cliff. But he walked right through the crowd and went on his way." Luke 4:28–30

I personally believe that He vanished. One moment there is an angry mob trying to grab Him and throw him off a cliff, yet He walks right through them, untouched. Maybe He put His hood over His head and *poof*, He suddenly disappeared! Well, maybe not exactly like that, but it was definitely a supernatural occurrence.

Jesus walked on the water a few times also (Mark 6:45–56; John 6:16–24). Mark and John write about the SAME incident, which took place right after the 5,000 were fed. (Mark 6:30-44; John 6:1-15)

John tells about when He walked through a locked door:

"On the evening of that first day of the week, when the disciples were together, with the doors locked for fear of the Jewish leaders, Jesus came and stood among them and said, 'Peace be with you!'" John 20:19

There are also many places where the Bible says, *"Jesus knew their thoughts ..."* (Matthew 9:4, Matthew 12:25, Luke 5:22, Luke 11:17). This has blown me away many times as I have pondered it.

For example, take a closer look at this story:

"One day as Jesus was standing by the Lake of Gennesaret, the people were crowding around him and listening to the word of God. He saw at the water's edge two boats, left there by the fishermen, who were washing their nets. He got into one of the boats, the one belonging to Simon, and asked him to put out a little from shore. Then he sat down and taught the people from the boat.

"When he had finished speaking, he said to Simon, 'Put out into deep water, and let down the nets for a catch.'

"Simon answered, 'Master, we've worked hard all night and haven't caught anything. But because you say so, I will let down the nets.'

"When they had done so, they caught such a large number of fish that their nets began to break. So they signaled their partners in the other boat to come and help them, and they came and filled both boats so full that they began to sink.

"When Simon Peter saw this, he fell at Jesus' knees and said, 'Go away from me, Lord; I am a sinful man!' For he and all his companions were astonished at the catch of fish they had taken, and so were James and John, the sons of Zebedee, Simon's partners.

"Then Jesus said to Simon, 'Don't be afraid; from now on you will fish for people.' So they pulled their boats up on shore, left everything and followed him." Luke 5:1–11

This story shows how Jesus knew people's thoughts and life stories. He knew that the disciples had not caught any fish. Through the Holy Spirit, He knew the disciples' hearts and needs, and that they had not caught any fish.

These are just a few of the things Jesus did. We serve an absolutely fascinating God! Get ready for quite a journey, because Jesus said you will do greater things:

"Very truly I tell you, whoever believes in me will do the works I have been doing, and they will do even greater things than these, because I am going to the Father." John 14:12

This does not mean just miracles; many people are comfortable with just miracles. *Greater things than these* means all the things that He did. I am inviting you on a journey that is going to change your life forever. In this book, I want to activate supernatural experiences in your life. But first, I need to lay a foundation.

The Foundation for All We Do

First of all, the main principle and purpose of experiencing the supernatural is found in Ephesians 1:17. This is actually the banner over my life and ministry. I have built all of my life's work in ministry on this foundation:

*"I keep asking that the God of our Lord Jesus Christ, the glorious Father, may give you the Spirit of wisdom and revelation, so **that you may know him better**."* Ephesians 1:17

All of our spiritual experiences, and everything that we do, is laid on the foundation of knowing God better. Do you know what this means? When it comes down to it, the thing we need most of all is godly character, humility and love. That is a rock–solid foundation that you can build an amazing house on that can support the weight of all kinds of things.

Love is the cornerstone of this foundation. Jesus said the greatest thing is to love others as He loves us. He reminds us through the apostle Paul that it all comes down to faith, hope and love—and the most important is love.

CHAPTER 3

WHY DO WE NOT HAVE SUPERNATURAL ENCOUNTERS?

There are a few reasons you might not be having supernatural encounters:

- Ignorance
- Fear of being deceived
- Cessationism
- Over–focus on the demonic
- Relying on logic, not the Spirit
- Fear of the supernatural
- Belief that experiences can only be earned through holiness

Ignorance and the Fear of Being Deceived

One of the most common reasons we do not have supernatural encounters is ignorance. People simply do not know that supernatural encounters can happen. For those who do, a big attack of the enemy right now is to cause a fear of being deceived.

This is a big attack of the enemy right now. This fear makes people pull back from listening for the Holy Spirit, and blocks them from feeling grace to step out and take a risk.

What if Peter felt that way? He would have never walked on water! What about Joseph, the father of Jesus? If he had not listened to the angel in his dream, he may not have taken Jesus and Mary to Egypt, and in the process, would not have saved Jesus' life. In both of these stories, Peter and Joseph took a risk and listened to what God was saying.

Cessationism Theology

From a theological standpoint, there is a doctrine called *Cessationism*, which basically teaches that supernatural gifts no longer exist and are not available to the Church. That means that the gifts of tongues, prophecy, healing, miracles and other supernatural experiences went away, or ceased, when the first apostles died.

Did you know that Cessationism, as a theology, has only been around since the early 20th century? Yet, in this short period of time, Cessationism has been responsible for many Christians no longer expecting to experience God and hear Him for themselves, which is sad.

Let me explain how this can happen. Unbelief often stops people from experiencing the supernatural. Jesus, Himself, could not do miracles around places that had concentrations of unbelief and a lack of faith. Unbelief can sometimes be due to bad theology—like the belief that God does not do these things anymore.

Does Cessationism even make sense? Let's look at what it says in Acts and consider this:

"In the last days, God says, I will pour out my Spirit on all people. Your sons and daughters will prophesy, your young men will see visions, your old men will dream dreams. Even on my servants, both men and women, I will pour out my Spirit in those days, and they will prophesy." Acts 2:17–18

If supernatural gifts and experiences went away, then how could all those people suddenly speak in other languages and prophecy (hear God's voice) like they did in Acts 2?

And why did Peter quote from the prophet Joel about what was happening that day? He was pointing out to them, and to us, that *the last days* had come. God is still pouring out His Spirit *on all people.*

I am simply saying that God is moving, right now, and is manifesting supernaturally on Earth in a new way.

Over-Focus on the Demonic

Another thing that has stopped us from hearing and encountering God is focusing too much on the demonic. Listen to me; I should ring a bell right now to get the Church's attention, because the Church has gotten so focused on the demonic instead of the Holy Spirit. We have ended up with a great big devil and a very small God. That will kill supernatural experiences!

We have turned into trouble-shooters. If we are always looking for trouble, then that is all we will see. This is tragic because we could be looking for people to bless instead of devils to curse.

Relying on Logic, Not the Spirit

Many Christians have developed a systematic way of thinking that over-focuses on logic at the expense of childlike faith. We have been conditioned to look and use our minds instead of our spirits. There is an almost cynical lack of wonder and trust that has crept in, working against faith in God—the same God who calls Himself a Father that *gives good gifts to those who ask.* This includes the Holy Spirit!

"Which of you fathers, if your son asks for a fish, will give him a snake instead? Or if he asks for an egg, will give

him a scorpion? If you then, though you are evil, know how to give good gifts to your children, how much more will your Father in heaven give the Holy Spirit to those who ask him!" Luke 11:11–13

"If you, then, though you are evil, know how to give good gifts to your children, how much more will your Father in heaven give good gifts to those who ask him!" Matthew 7:11

Fear of the Supernatural

There are those who simply fear the supernatural realm. Many people had nightmares as kids or watched horror movies that caused them to grow up fearing everything supernatural. That was me. I was afraid to even see an angel for a long time. Children's nightmares are an attack of Satan to cause them to grow up so afraid of the supernatural side of God that they do not want anything to do with it or God.

Intimacy vs. Holiness

Let's talk about intimacy versus holiness. This is another reason why we have not experienced the supernatural in the way that God has provided for us. There has been a recent surge of teaching where people are focusing on the holiness of God and trying to eliminate sin from their lives. Now, this is good, but do you know what?

You are probably never going to fully eliminate sin from your life. If you focus too much on trying to become holy by avoiding sin, then that is all you are going to see—sin.

It is not easy to explain, but this type of focus can actually distract you from understanding God's grace and love. It can even distract you from having eyes to see spiritual things happening around you.

Now let me bring balance to this so you understand what I am trying to say: we can start thinking that we are not getting any visitations because of the sin in our lives. But if we confess our sins, He is faithful and will forgive us.

"If we confess our sins, he is faithful and just and will forgive us our sins and purify us from all unrighteousness." 1 John 1:9

There is grace and your sins go under the blood of Jesus. There may be some particular cases, but sin issues are not usually holding you back. A more likely scenario is that you have lacked training and have not learned to discern what God is already saying. You might just not know how to hear yet.

I want to encourage you to focus on intimacy with God rather than holiness. I want you to become holy, of course, but do not focus on that. Focus on being intimate and the holiness will follow along nicely. It is a fruit of spending time with Him.

The Other Extreme: Over-Focus on Spiritual Experiences

I have seen an over-focus on wanting an *experience* in charismatic prophetic communities. On this side of the extreme, an emphasis is placed on having a visitation. Then we start feeling disappointed or left out, or we believe that there is something wrong with us if we do not have an experience.

For those who can relate, start by developing the ability to know Him better. That is going to jump-start you into the Spirit of wisdom and revelation. This is an invitation for you right now to move into seeing and understanding the deeper things of God through the Holy Spirit.

I want to pray right now to break all of this stuff off:

We take this right now—all of this unbelief, focusing too much on the demonic, over-focus on logic, fear of the supernatural—and we break these off now in Jesus' name. Also, if you have struggled with any of these issues, I pray right now for an opening of your spirit, in Jesus' name.

Let me tell you—although I have a lot of supernatural experiences, it was not always that way. In fact, I had to develop it, learn to discern, and then create a way to help others.

That is why I am training people. I want to teach you to go deeper. But do you know something? I would give up all the encounters and experiences for one good day on the couch with Jesus. Really. When it comes down to it, loving God and loving people is really what matters.

CHAPTER 4

WE CAN LEARN TO DISCERN

How Do You Learn to Discern?

What do I mean by learning to discern? You know, learning to discern is something that the Lord spoke to me about a long time ago.

Why learn? Because we have to apply ourselves in order to understand supernatural things. We have to understand how it works.

Years ago, I was sitting at a table between two amazing men of God who I did not know personally at the time. It turned out that the prophet Bob Jones was on one side of me and Rick Joyner, founder of MorningStar Ministries and author of *The Final Quest* as well as over fifty other books, was on the other side of me.

I was sitting there thinking to myself that I had a burning question. At that time, I used to write down my questions for when I had a chance to get around seasoned people who could possibly answer them for me.

My Burning Question

I was thinking about Bob Jones' *Shepherd's Rod* books and Rick Joyner's epic visions in his book, *The Final Quest*. I wondered how they get all those words and insights from God.

My burning question was, "How did Rick get all those prophetic visions, anyway?" There are all sorts of symbols and visions in that book, and it is like reading a novel that has obvious spiritual insight and direction. I wanted to ask Rick, "Did you see it? Was it a dream? Was it an open vision? Were they panoramic pictures in your mind? Did the Holy Spirit speak to you? Were you actually taken there, or what?"

Okay, maybe it was more than one question, but you get the idea. I was so hungry for understanding. And here is the cool thing about the supernatural: while I was literally thinking those things, but had not yet said a word, Bob Jones leaned over to me and answered my questions! He said in his unique *Bob Jones way*, "Well boy, once you understand how God speaks, then it does not matter how it came to you."

In the years since that conversation, I have found that sometimes God speaks while I am dreaming and sometimes He is more dramatic. Other times, I get pictures in my mind. However God chooses to speak to me, I value it all.

Practice Hearing God

I have experiences all the time. If you have been following my prophetic words for any number of years, I seem to average about five encounters a month, and during certain times of the year, they increase beyond that. They are not all high-level, dramatic encounters; some come in dreams and some come in that still, small voice. It really does not matter, because here is the point: I have learned to *practice paying attention.*

Did you know that we need to practice hearing God? We practice preaching, teaching, administration and worship. We practice every gift except the prophetic—the seeing and hearing spiritually part—which really needs to come back into play and into our focus. What is practice? The Bible calls it *constant use:*

*"But solid food is for the mature, who by **constant use** have trained themselves to distinguish good from evil."* Hebrews 5:14

Now, *practicing* will help deal with the fear of being deceived. Constant use of our spiritual gifts will fix this issue. Learn to discern and you will not be duped!

God Conceals Things

Did you know that God is a concealing God? Just look at His nature. Job 33 talks about dreams and how God speaks:

"For God may speak in one way, or in another, yet man does not perceive it. In a dream, in a vision of the night, when deep sleep falls upon men, while slumbering on their beds, then He opens the ears of men, and seals their instruction. In order to turn man from his deed, and conceal pride from man, He keeps back his soul from the pit, and his life from perishing by the sword." Job 33:14–18 NKJV

Wow! God is speaking all the time, yet we may not perceive it. I have underlined those verses in my Bible. He is always speaking, but we may not understand. And then there are other times when He conceals His voice from our awareness.

God may impart revelation directly into your spirit. For example, you know you had a dream, but you do not remember, or you have an encounter that you do not understand. Our concealing God does this so that, later on, He can bypass your logical, natural mind and keep you from acting out of pride.

When God conceals His voice, He is also protecting you from spiritual warfare. The enemy will not bother to attack you when you get this type of revelation. God does this all the time, so do not be discouraged if you do not always remember or understand. God does seal them for our good.

Parables: God's Hidden Language

God often uses a type of hidden language. I know, this can sound mystical and spooky. But if we want to be naturally supernatural, we need to grab hold of God's language and learn it.

People say, "All this sounds exclusive." You know, it may sound that way, but these are Jesus' words:

"The disciples came to him and asked, 'Why do you speak to the people in parables?' He replied, 'Because the knowledge of the secrets of the kingdom of heaven has been given to you, but not to them. Whoever has will be given more, and they will have an abundance. Whoever does not have, even what they have will be taken from them. This is why I speak to them in parables: 'Though seeing, they do not see; though hearing, they do not hear or understand.''' Matthew 13:10–13

Wow! Why did Jesus speak to the people in parables? Because these are stories about the Kingdom. The knowledge of the secrets of the Kingdom is given to those who believe. It is not for people who do not believe.

Jesus said, *"Whoever has will be given more, and they will have an abundance. Whoever does not have, even what they have will be taken from them"* (Matthew 13:12). This is why Jesus taught using parables.

"Though seeing they do not see; though hearing they do not hear or understand." Matthew 13:13

In other words, Jesus is saying that we need to get eyes to see and ears to hear. This is something He said often.

"Ears that hear and eyes that see—the Lord has made them both." Proverbs 20:12

He was teaching through parables all of the time, talking about getting those eyes to see. That is the knowledge of the secrets of the Kingdom of Heaven. These are principles that will give you more.

The Importance of Valuing His Voice

Remember, He said that whoever has this wisdom, knowledge and understanding of God's language will be given more.

So, what is the condition of people today? Do you know what? It is the same as in Jesus' day. Sadly, people do not have the knowledge or understanding they need. They stopped valuing these things, so what they had was taken from them.

You have to grab hold of this. It is as easy as getting back into valuing the supernatural. Then it will start in abundance again. In fact, it will be overflowing. Dreams are like night parables. When we stop valuing revelation, we will stop receiving it until we value it again.

Our condition today is a sign that we have gotten into our natural minds instead of our spirits. We have valued teaching above revelation and the supernatural—instead of holding them both in high regard, because both reveal God's heart.

"It is the glory of God to conceal things, but the glory of kings is to search things out." Proverbs 25:2 ESV

God is into concealing a matter. His nature is to conceal or hide things. I think it is like a lover's game. He wants you to run after Him.

There are spiritual principles in the Bible that will work no matter who uses them. That is why Jesus said they have been hidden from those who do not believe. Today people are actually discovering these things, and are activating them without a relationship with God. They will not be as effective as we are with a relationship with God through Jesus, though the principles will still work to some degree.

God wants to build a desire in you, and then meet that desire so He can draw you closer. To do that, He may give you an experience. When I have an experience, do you know what I have realized? It causes me to search the matter out.

The Journey of Searching Things Out

When we search things out, it causes us to start a journey. God knows this about me and you. He can drop a dream into me, and He knows that I am going to go searching. I am going to be researching on the Internet and doing a word study.

A lot of times I find out what the hidden meaning is and I think, "Wow, that was not all that powerful." But then Jesus says, "Yeah, but how great was that journey? You know, you just spent a lot of time in My Word."

He would use this invitation from Him like a carrot to lead me along, like a lover's game, to take me deeper. He really wants to open up the mysteries of the secrets of the Kingdom of God over us.

I want to restore this lost art. Jesus said that knowledge, parables, eyes to see and ears to hear will all be given to us. All we need to do right now is to start valuing them.

Develop your ability to recognize how God is speaking through symbolism. When you do this consistently, you will be given more. This is why I journal every day. I want to pay attention to what I am seeing.

I am not saying you have to journal every day, but I want to invite you into the practice of it. Do you know what? You are taking in a ministry-level message here. If you are not writing things down, it could be one of the reasons you are not getting anything else. When you begin to write things down, you will value and cherish them. Search the matter out and you will start to get more.

We want to gain deeper understanding. In Matthew 13, Jesus addressed the fact that we have to develop the ability to use our Holy Spirit interpretive skills.

Look at the ways Daniel developed his ability to hear God:

"Inasmuch as an excellent spirit, knowledge, understanding, interpreting dreams, solving riddles, and explaining enigmas were found in this Daniel, whom the king named Belteshazzar, now let Daniel be called, and he will give the interpretation." Daniel 5:12 NKJV

Wow, how about you? Is that in you? I know that I actually have that Joseph and Daniel "interpreting dreams" anointing.

I do not think I was born with this gift because I did not understand my dreams for a number of years. But I began to learn from and be trained by other people. I studied and eventually began to teach biblical dream interpretation to others.

All you have to do is study God's hidden language to understand the deeper meanings of things like riddles, mysteries and parables. If you do, life parables are going to come alive to you.

Developing Your Spiritual Senses

God is raising up seers right now as well as hearers. I have been training people in the prophetic in ministry schools for a long time, and I have noticed that most of us have eyes to see only in the natural. From an early age, most people have only learned to think logically. We need to break out of the Western mindset that says, "Show me the money," or "I will believe it when I see it."

Another thing I have noticed is that most people think they should listen to God speak internally to their spirit, like words in their mind. Others believe that the Holy

Spirit only speaks to you word-for-word, so there is no need for interpretation. Pretty much everyone has been trained to think that when we receive something from God, we have to repeat it back word-for-word. This is good, but it is not the only way God speaks.

Prophecies, dreams, visions, supernatural encounters and life parables—these are all ways He speaks. Most people are just using their spiritual ears and have not been trained to use the rest of their spiritual senses—hearing, smelling, tasting, feeling, seeing and understanding the spiritual realm—through the Holy Spirit.

I am a seer, but that does not necessarily mean I only see visions. I have all of my receptors open to seeing, hearing, feeling and so forth. A true seer cannot be shut down because if their ability to see is shut down, they will always be able to perceive another way.

Jeremiah was an amazing seer and prophet:

"The word of the Lord came to me and He said, 'What do you see, Jeremiah?'

"'I see the branch of an almond tree,' I replied. The Lord said to me, 'You have seen correctly, for I am watching to see that my word is fulfilled.'" Jeremiah 1:11–12

Modern-Day Parables

Now, check this out. The Hebrew word for almond tree actually rhymes with the Hebrew word for watching. This is an example of God speaking to Jeremiah through something like a parable, or really more like a play on words. Jeremiah could not only hear; he could also see.

Have you ever had a friend who loves to tell jokes filled with puns? Sometimes you may not even understand the joke or pun until you think about it for a while. Then it hits you, and you see the play on words.

It is a similar dynamic at times with God. Just like your friend's face fills with delight when you finally get it, God is delighted when we ponder His message until we get it. It is interesting to note that He is doing this right now all the time on the news.

Some examples of modern-day parables are: if you get a new pickup truck in a dream, then things are about to *pick up* for you; if you spill ketchup in a dream (even in real life), then you are playing *catch up* right now. Those are some possible modern-day understandings. If you would like more training on dreams online, we offer *The Dream Crash Course* and my *Understand Your Dreams Now* book.

CHAPTER 5

GOING DEEPER THROUGH PRACTICE

Tips to Go Deeper

To get deeper spiritual insight, you will need to track all the ways that God speaks to you by writing it down. It does not matter if you use a paper journal or a computer journal. Use something, for crying out loud! Do something that fits you. Do not try to be like me—be like you.

You will need to sift through your experiences. I journal on a computer so that I can search for topics based on key words to see if I have had a certain dream or experience before. For example, I may remember something God spoke, but I need to recall the context or more of the details.

Also, study the dreams, metaphors and symbolism in the Bible. All you have to do to begin is look up *dream* or *vision* in the Bible. Read the books of Daniel and Ezekiel and the encounters that people had throughout the Bible.

Matthew 13 is another good place to learn the symbolic meanings of everyday things.

Do spiritual activations by starting somewhere simple, like reading your Bible and listening to what God is saying, or maybe sharing a prophetic word you are hearing with someone else. I do this daily.

I am a seasoned prophet now. I have been doing prophetic ministry for almost twenty-five years. But, I still do the daily stuff. I still journal. I still send words out on Facebook and Twitter. I will take a prophetic word or an encouragement to someone outside of my comfort zone.

My office used to be in a co-working environment near Venice Beach so I could be around a wide variety of people. I would get an encouraging word for someone and share it. I work on activating these things in my life every single day. When you begin doing these small steps, it will not take long before your gifts begin to explode in your life.

Embracing the Fundamentals

When I was a kid, I was invited to go to basketball camp. I was a tall kid, but I was not good at basketball. I thought we were going to learn really cool stuff. Do you know what they focused on? You guessed it: the fundamentals.

We learned to pass, dribble and shoot. *Pass, dribble, and shoot.* We covered the basics over and over. I have learned that doing the basics over and over will open spiritual things up to you as well.

If you want to increase your ability to see spiritually, you will need to break away from the Western, logical mindset. It causes spiritual dullness so that the very first thing you experience is doubt instead of belief.

Create an environment of belief around you. Clean doubt and unbelief from your spiritual lenses so you can have eyes to see. Remove critical judgment from your thinking and your way of seeing others.

This is so important! If you have been around my ministry, you know my heart for this. A major, personal breakthrough happened when I broke through having a judgmental focus.

Whether you are learning these things for the first time or are seasoned at it, start sharing what you see and hear with others. Begin to step out. Of course, you will need to learn to recognize whether biblical principles support what you see, hear and experience.

I am a seer, so I drive pastors and teachers crazy because sometimes I say what I see before I understand it.

They ask me, "Where is that in the Bible?" I have to look it up later. I really do. I know that if it does not violate a biblical principle, then we are good.

It is important to understand that people are afraid of being deceived. They wonder, "Is this from Satan or from an angel?" Fear is a negative spirit that can hold us down. Studying the Bible will help renew our minds and allow our hearts to overcome fear and trust God no matter how He speaks.

Are We Testing or Judging a Word?

Many people do not know the difference between testing a word to find out if it is good as opposed to judging the word with a critical spirit. They do not know the difference. Knowing the difference comes with practice.

Meditate on this Bible verse:

"But solid food is for the mature, who by constant use have trained themselves to distinguish good from evil." Hebrews 5:14

If I get a prophetic word or I release prophetic words on my blog, some contain a lot of Bible verses and others do not. Some are from my personal experiences, some are not. If you have a critical spirit, the first thing you might find yourself asking is, "Where is that in the Bible?" A critical spirit will cause you to doubt before you believe. I am not saying to believe everything, but do not doubt before you test it. There is a difference.

The way to get out of that critical judgment so you can open up and create faith is to search out the matter for yourself first. If nothing else, you can search on the Internet! If you do not understand the Bible well enough yet to know these principles, that is the best starting place for you.

For example, when someone gets healed or has a supernatural encounter, like gold dust or gemstones falling into a meeting, the first thing many people do is doubt as opposed to believing. Granted, these are challenging phenomena to our minds. But we need to open up that belief system and say, "Yes, God! Yes to opening up our belief to what You are doing. We say yes, God, to opening the supernatural over us. Help us with our unbelief!"

Angels and the Supernatural

Have you ever had spiritual experiences, such as dreams from God, visions or angelic encounters? In a recent course that I taught on this topic, the vast majority had experienced some dreams, about half had things happen that they could not explain, and a decent number were experiencing dreams and visions on a regular basis. The smallest percentage had never experienced the supernatural. Remember, it does not mean anything bad or that something is wrong if you have not experienced these kinds of things.

That is fine because that is going to change.

Listen, if you tend to have more encounters, it does not make you a better Christian. And if you have not had many encounters, God does not love you any less. He loves you where you are.

We need to grab hold of God's love. You know, He is for you. He is not against you. It does not make you any more mature if you are having supernatural encounters.

Do not feel left out. It could be that you just have some things coming against you, but this would only be because you have a high calling.

Supernatural Experiences

Sometimes supernatural experiences can be dramatic, and at other times they can be quite natural or even seem coincidental.

Because I did not have a lot of formal training about God's supernatural ways, I know first-hand how important it is to learn from people who understand supernatural things. I had to learn through personal experiences and asking questions when I was around experienced teachers and leaders.

I want to train you so that you will not have to take the long road like I did. We do not hear very often about the importance of spiritual training, so I will cover it here.

We need to understand these things. Sometimes you can just *know* that God is saying something. Maybe another time you sense an angel is there. Sometimes it is more dramatic or obvious so, as I have been saying, you will need to take notes.

Practice discerning. I keep repeating this because it is important that your spirit is sensitive to the atmosphere around you. Even after all these years, I still take notes after every meeting. I attended or helped lead one hundred and fifty meetings a year for ten years, and I would still take notes!

I still take notes now because that is how I train myself to discern. For example, I want to know what types of angels are in the room because I do not always see them with my eyes. Most of the time they are cloaked (hidden), but they are there.

When Your Life Is the Message

I have a gift that most people do not understand. It really is a supernatural thing, but it takes getting used to. It is this process of *living out* prophetic words. I felt God tell me to include this because there are people reading this book that need this understanding.

Many prophets of the Bible like Jeremiah, Isaiah and Hosea, to name a few, had this type of gift. The events in their personal lives became a parable or prophetic message for others.

You may be gifted this way, and the message can be for your community, yourself or a combination of both. It does not happen with everyone, and it takes discernment and wisdom to understand it.

I often live out prophetic words over a person, church, city or other situation. For example, I tend to live out the prophetic words that I release monthly. They contain elements of things that happen to me, and the situations have meaning beyond the surface.

This particular gift requires that I have a high level of spiritual sensitivity. When I travel, I cannot stay in people's homes and rest because I get attacked by the demonic assignment that is against them. I do not have spiritual authority to oppose demonic assignments in another person's home, but I can release angels over them. I can rest better in hotels because I do have spiritual authority to shut down negative things in my own room.

My gift involves having spiritual authority to release others from things that are stopping them and holding them back. Even if you are at a level like Billy Graham, God will show me if there is something in your family line that is stopping you from moving to a new level.

That is called a *living parable* and it is important to recognize these things because when it occurs, it can blow you away if you do not discern what is happening.

Here is an example of how I live a parable. I was going to Canada to minister and my wife said, "Hey look. I have $6.00 in Canadian coins that I have been saving since your last trip." So I took the coins and headed to the airport. On the plane, I noticed that I was in seat number 6 on both flights. I arrived at gate 66, and my hosts took me to a new Motel 6. I kept seeing all these sixes.

It is not unusual for people to immediately think 666 means something bad. But the Holy Spirit spoke to me that the church I was speaking at had forgotten a promise from six years ago. Sure enough there was a forgotten promise, and we were able to bring that promise forward. That is why God was speaking through all the sixes!

That was not the only living parable I had on that trip. I was on a short flight, and yet the airline lost my luggage. Now, I have angels that protect my travel and luggage, so I have never missed a meeting because of missing a flight or losing luggage. So, when my luggage does get lost it is usually a prophetic message. I knew in this case that there was something dear to this congregation that they were about to lose if they waited.

I arrived on Sunday morning, and at the last minute I heard God say, "If they wait and do not settle for less ..." The pastor picked me up at the airport and said it was an hour and a half drive to the hotel. An hour and a half later, I sensed God telling me share these living parable stories. I had just met the guy!

So we looked up and realized that we were driving in the wrong direction. We went the wrong way! He looked at me and said, "No way." I said, "Yes, way. Listen, you could be tempted to go the wrong way."

Sure enough, the pastor told me that they were taking the prophetic out of the church and becoming seeker sensitive. There is nothing wrong with this if it is your calling, like Joel Osteen, who has an anointing for it. But doing it to increase your membership or something like that is the wrong way.

My Current Message to the Church

Another life parable that I am living through is a message that the body of Christ is sick. As I write this, I have been sick for three years due to attacks from the occult and from Christians who have been praying against me because of things I have been doing and sharing. The prophetic word I have been living out is that the Church is suffering from spiritual, physical, mental and emotional sickness because of judgments.

You can learn to recognize when you are living out a prophetic word. Ask God to speak to you through natural, everyday things. Then notice when things are starting to go wrong or are out of the ordinary. Look for symbolic meaning as they happen. Begin to notice the news and events in your community. What is the deeper prophetic message in each of these?

Not everything is a prophetic message, but God is speaking all the time and He will confirm what He is saying. The more you develop this, the more you will understand it.

Even Jesus lived out prophetic words. There are two instances in the Bible where storms came to kill Jesus and

His disciples. The prophetic message was how to respond in the storms of life.

In Mark 4, the enemy wanted to kill them by capsizing their boat. Jesus slept in the belly of the boat while the storm raged to show us that we can rest, and even sleep, in the midst of life's storms.

"That day when evening came, he said to his disciples, 'Let us go over to the other side.' Leaving the crowd behind, they took him along, just as he was, in the boat. There were also other boats with him. A furious squall came up, and the waves broke over the boat, so that it was nearly swamped. Jesus was in the stern, sleeping on a cushion. The disciples woke him and said to him, 'Teacher, don't you care if we drown?'

"He got up, rebuked the wind and said to the waves, 'Quiet! Be still!' Then the wind died down and it was completely calm.

"He said to his disciples, 'Why are you so afraid? Do you still have no faith?'

"They were terrified and asked each other, 'Who is this? Even the wind and the waves obey him!'" Mark 4:35–41

In Matthew 14, Jesus rose above the storm and walked on the water. He invited Peter—and us—to join Him.

"Immediately Jesus made the disciples get into the boat and go on ahead of him to the other side, while he dismissed the crowd. After he had dismissed them, he went up on a mountainside by himself to pray. Later that night, he was there alone, and the boat was already a considerable distance from land, buffeted by the waves because the wind was against it.

"Shortly before dawn Jesus went out to them, walking on the lake. When the disciples saw him walking on the lake, they were terrified. 'It's a ghost,' they said, and cried out in fear.

"But Jesus immediately said to them: 'Take courage! It is I. Don't be afraid.'

"'Lord, if it's you,' Peter replied, 'tell me to come to you on the water.'

"'Come,' he said.

"Then Peter got down out of the boat, walked on the water and came toward Jesus. But when he saw the wind, he was afraid and, beginning to sink, cried out, 'Lord, save me!'

"Immediately Jesus reached out his hand and caught him. 'You of little faith,' he said, 'why did you doubt?'

"And when they climbed into the boat, the wind died down. Then those who were in the boat worshiped him, saying, 'Truly you are the Son of God.'

"When they had crossed over, they landed at Gennesaret. And when the men of that place recognized Jesus, they sent word to all the surrounding country. People brought all their sick to him and begged him to let the sick just touch the edge of his cloak, and all who touched it were healed." Matthew 14:22–36

Those were prophetic signs. There are all kinds of them that we can see in the Bible and in our everyday lives.

Seeing Demons but Not Angels?

This is a topic that comes up frequently. If I were to say, "There is an angel in the room," so many people would doubt it—*especially* if I said it on Sunday morning.

I can sense the type of angels that are in a church. When I tell people about the angels I see around them, I am often met with doubt and unbelief. They even wonder if I am New Age. Do you know what? This is not good because if I were to tell the same crowd that there was a demon in the room, there would be more people willing to believe me than if I had said that there was an angel present!

This shows that Christians have become over-focused on the demonic and deliverance, and not focused enough on angels and the goodness of God. We have trained ourselves to see what is wrong with people and our environment, and we have become negativity *troubleshooters*. We end up shooting things down as opposed to grabbing hold of what is right. We need to switch over to seeing angels instead of the demonic. We need to focus more on the gifts, calling and destiny in people instead of what is going wrong with them.

Have you noticed that the Bible gives a lot more attention to encounters that emphasize the power of God, Jesus, and the Holy Spirit than attention to the demonic realm? I challenge you to look this up. How many times do you see Jesus talking about the demonic realm? Very little! One time He called Peter *Satan*—remember, *Get behind Me Satan!*—but otherwise, He focused on the demonic very little.

If anything, Jesus spent His time telling demons to either be quiet or to leave. The apostle Paul did not talk about the demonic stronghold over Ephesus, the city that revered the Temple of Diana. Both Jesus and Paul focused on God's goodness and concern for people.

"Finally, brothers and sisters, whatever is true, whatever is noble, whatever is right, whatever is pure, whatever is lovely, whatever is admirable—if anything is excellent or praiseworthy—think about such things." Philippians 4:8

Somehow we have gotten over-focused on the demonic. You know, it takes practice to keep looking for the good and to stop listening for demons. Demons are liars, which is why I do not listen to them. You will want to listen to angels if you want to see the truth.

Father, I pray right now for this shift over people, because this needs to happen. There is a gift of being able to know what is going on, called discerning of spirits. The gift of being able to discern is a good thing, but we have to learn what the opposite is and what to shift over people. Help us to see and affirm the goodness of God over their lives as we shift away from the darkness, in Jesus' name.

CHAPTER 6

KEEPING A KINGDOM FOCUS: ANGELS

Steps to Seeing More Angels

I used to see demons all the time, so I am not judgmental of people who do. I used to have to close my spiritual eyes due to the demonic until I learned to pray and change my focus. It is okay to recognize the demonic attack against a person, but I have learned that listening to a demon speak or getting attacked by them is not productive.

Instead, begin to ask God to show you the angels in a situation rather than the demons. When demons do speak, stop listening to them. Take note of when you see angels or sense angels and then pray and ask God to activate the angelic. It can look as simple as something like this, "God, open my eyes so that I can see."

When you do see something negative over a person—for instance, the spirit of suicide, sickness or death—that is a spiritual gift called *discernment of spirits*. If you come into agreement with those negative things over a person by telling them, "Hey, you know, you have suicide on you," that will not be very productive.

You need to tell them *why* they have it so that they can get free from it. What positive life calling or angel is assigned to them? You have to be able to see the rest of the picture so you can help free them.

Many people with the discernment of spirits gift have not been trained, so they might say, "Well, I cannot lie." True, we do not want to lie. But we also do not want to come into agreement with the darkness over them. We need to learn how to see the opposite. I call this *flipping it*. Flip it, and flip it good! I cover this more in many of the other materials available through my website.

In 1991, I had a radical encounter with an angel while camping at Big Sur. I was literally thrown to the ground by the angel's presence. Now, I did not actually see the angel with my eyes, but make no mistake—I could *see* it. This was my first radical encounter. I felt the presence and power of God there. I can still hear word-for-word the message the angle spoke into my spirit. Thirteen years later, all the things the angel told me came to pass and I released it as a prophetic word in my book, *Divine Alliances*, which is about marriages, ministries and businesses coming together for the Kingdom of God.

I want to encourage you to grab hold of these deeper things; do not dismiss them because you do not understand them. God is outside of time. This is the timing gift, and it has to do with seasons as well.

I am a *times and seasons* prophetic person. Because God is outside of time, we tend to think that everything we hear pertains to a certain timeframe. Most people miss this when interpreting prophetic words and experiences.

Throughout history, people have thought Jesus would return *any minute now*, or that He already did and they missed it. They were repeatedly mistaken because they did not understand timing. I want to write a book someday called, *Jesus Has Not Come Back Yet. Now What?* We are focusing too much on Jesus coming back instead of doing the work of the Kingdom.

Angelic Encounters in the Early Church

Peter had an encounter with an angel in Acts 12, but he did not realize what was happening to him. It is the same with us; sometimes we know and sometimes we do not.

God is outside of time, so the Holy Spirit and angels will speak to us in ways that are outside of our paradigms. This can lead to misunderstanding.

Many people think that everything is from Jesus. But do you know what? There is the Father, the Son and the Holy Spirit. And then there are angels. A biblical example of this is in Acts, where Philip has an encounter with an Ethiopian eunuch:

*"**Now an angel of the Lord said to Philip**, 'Go south to the road—the desert road—that goes down from Jerusalem to Gaza.' So he started out, and on his way he met an Ethiopian eunuch, an important official in charge of all the treasury of the Kandake (which means 'queen of the Ethiopians'). This man had gone to Jerusalem to worship, and on his way home was sitting in his chariot reading the Book of Isaiah the prophet. **The Spirit told Philip**, 'Go to that chariot and stay near it.' Then Philip ran up to the chariot and heard the man reading Isaiah the prophet. 'Do you understand what you are reading?' Philip asked."* Acts 8:26–30

In Acts 8:26, the angel spoke to Philip; in Acts 8:29, the Spirit told Philip to go stand next to the chariot. He starts out with an angel speaking to him, and when he got there the Holy Spirit spoke. Apparently, Philip knew the difference.

Acts 12 tells of another encounter Peter had:

"The night before Herod was to bring him to trial, Peter was sleeping between two soldiers, bound with two chains, and sentries stood guard at the entrance. Suddenly an angel of the Lord appeared and a light shone in the cell. He struck Peter on the side and woke him up. 'Quick, get up!' he said, and the chains fell off Peter's wrists.

"Then the angel said to him, 'Put on your clothes and sandals.' And Peter did so. 'Wrap your cloak around you and follow me,' the angel told him.

"Peter followed him out of the prison, but he had no idea that what the angel was doing was really happening; he thought he was seeing a vision.

"They passed the first and second guards and came to the iron gate leading to the city. It opened for them by itself, and they went through it. When they had walked the length of one street, suddenly the angel left him." Acts 12:6–10

Peter had been arrested. He was *bound with two chains* and there were people at the door. Suddenly an angel of the Lord appeared and struck Peter, waking him up, and said, *"Quick, get up! Put on your clothes and sandals. Wrap your cloak around you …"* It sounds like a mom: "Get dressed, get your shoes, get your coat. Let's get out of here!"

*"Peter followed him out of the prison, **but he had no idea that what the angel was doing was really happening …**"*
Acts 12:9

Mark that in your Bible. He had no idea what was actually happening. Peter did realize it was an angel, but not that it was actually happening and not just a vision.

The story continues:

"They passed the first and second guards and came to the iron gate leading to the city. It opened for them by itself, and they went through it.

"When they had walked the length of one street, suddenly the angel left him. Then Peter came to himself and said, 'Now I know without a doubt that the Lord has sent his angel and rescued me from Herod's clutches and from everything the Jewish people were hoping would happen.'

"When this had dawned on him, he went to the house of Mary the mother of John, also called Mark, where many people had gathered and were praying. Peter knocked at the outer entrance, and a servant named Rhoda came to answer the door. When she recognized Peter's voice, she was so overjoyed she ran back without opening it and exclaimed, 'Peter is at the door!'

'You're out of your mind,' they told her. When she kept insisting that it was so, they said, 'It must be his angel.' But Peter kept on knocking, and when they opened the door and saw him, they were astonished." Acts 12:10–16

When the iron prison gates opened, Peter came to himself and said, "*Now, I know without a doubt that the Lord has sent His angel and rescued me.*" Sometimes you can have an encounter and you think it is a vision but it is actually happening.

When he realized this, Peter went to Mary's house, where the disciples were praying for him. A girl saw Peter at the door and reported back, "Peter is at the door!" They said, "You are out of your mind." They would not listen, and when she kept insisting they concluded, "It must be his angel."

Have you ever thought about that? They did not all run to the door and say, "Oh my goodness, Peter's angel is at the door!"

The fact that they were so ready to believe it was Peter's angel is an indicator that angelic encounters were common, and that we all have angels that can look just like us. We need to get back to expecting angelic encounters as the norm.

Here is another encounter from Acts 10:

*"At Caesarea there was a man named Cornelius, a centurion in what was known as the Italian Regiment. He and all his family were devout and God-fearing; he gave generously to those in need and prayed to God regularly. One day at about three in the afternoon he had a vision. **He distinctly saw an angel of God**, who came to him and said, 'Cornelius!'"* Acts 10:1–3

The Bible says that Cornelius distinctly saw an angel. He was a Gentile who believed in God, but had not yet heard the gospel. But he was ready to believe the things God showed him. It is possible that this was the first time he had seen an angel that also talked to him. His encounter was significant in that it became a catalyst introducing the gospel of Jesus, not only to his household but to all races of people.

CHAPTER 7

IS IT FROM GOD EVEN IF IT IS WEIRD?

Strange Experiences

The books of Daniel, Revelation and Ezekiel contain some strange events with God. I invite you to read them to see examples of God speaking in various ways. People ask me, "What was the purpose of that?" Or they say, "Well, I heard this voice that said, 'Go pick the hay.' What was that about, Doug?" It might have been God, or an angel may have visited them.

Another question people ask me is, "What was the purpose for the angel standing in my room?" Sometimes, the purpose is simply God giving you a glimpse into the supernatural realm that is all around you because He wants to connect with you.

Maybe God is showing you that He cares about you, and He is demonstrating His delight in you. We do not always know. It is difficult to understand things at times;

there is not always a logical reason. But that is okay. Remember, God is outside of time and logic.

Let's look again at Acts 8, with Philip and the Ethiopian:

"As they traveled along the road, they came to some water and the eunuch said, 'Look, here is water. What can stand in the way of my being baptized?' And he gave orders to stop the chariot. Then both Philip and the eunuch went down into the water and Philip baptized him. **When they came up out of the water, the Spirit of the Lord suddenly took Philip away, and the eunuch did not see him again,** *but went on his way rejoicing. Philip, however, appeared at Azotus and traveled about, preaching the gospel in all the towns until he reached Caesarea."* Acts 8:36–40

When Philip came up out of the water after baptizing the Ethiopian, he suddenly found himself in another city. That was a *transportation*: he was transported from one place on Earth to another. This also happened to Elijah. What a strange occurrence!

There was also a time Peter fell into a trance:

"About noon the following day as they were on their journey and approaching the city, Peter went up on the roof to pray. He became hungry and wanted something to eat, and while the meal was being prepared, he fell into a trance. He saw heaven opened and something like a large sheet being let

down to earth by its four corners. It contained all kinds of four-footed animals, as well as reptiles and birds. Then a voice told him, 'Get up, Peter. Kill and eat.'

"'Surely not, Lord!' Peter replied. 'I have never eaten anything impure or unclean.' The voice spoke to him a second time, **'Do not call anything impure that God has made clean.'** This happened three times, and immediately the sheet was taken back to heaven." Acts 10:9–16

Peter went up on the roof to pray. God wanted to radically change his understanding and his theology, so He took Peter into a trance and spoke to him. When the sheet came down with *unclean* animals on it, God said, *"Get up, Peter. Kill and eat."* God was using the trance to release new understanding into Peter.

What about the End Times?

I believe that we are entering into a new time. We do not truly understand the end times. We have tried to make sense of the end times with an old wineskin mindset, and this will not work.

It is not until the visions of Daniel and the book of Revelation are opened to us in a supernatural way that we will actually understand these things. This is why I gave up trying to understand end times. I would be getting out of line and out of timing. There are some things that still need to really come about for us to accurately understand those things.

It took a supernatural encounter for Peter to understand that the gospel was also for the Gentiles. We need to clear our spiritual atmospheres and create the open heavens that will allow for experiences with God that unlock important revelations.

CHAPTER 8

WHAT IS AN OPEN HEAVEN?

"The Lord will open the heavens, the storehouse of his bounty, to send rain on your land in season and to bless all the work of your hands. You will lend to many nations but will borrow from none." Deuteronomy 28:12

The Bible talks about an *open heaven* over your work and your money. God said He wants to open the heavens, the storehouse of His bounty, and send rain (symbolic for blessings) on your land in season and bless all the work of your hands. This can happen to you, by the way, even in a *famine* of economic downturns and unemployment:

"Now there was a famine in the land—besides the previous famine in Abraham's time—and Isaac went to Abimelek king of the Philistines in Gerar. The Lord appeared to Isaac and said, 'Do not go down to Egypt; live in the land where I tell you to live. Stay in this land for a while, and I will be with you and will bless you ...'

"Isaac planted crops in that land and the same year reaped a hundredfold, because the Lord blessed him. The man became

rich, and his wealth continued to grow until he became very wealthy. He had so many flocks and herds and servants that the Philistines envied him." Genesis 26:1–3, 12–14

God can speak to you more clearly in an open heaven. Isaac got blessed in the year of the famine. He planted a crop and it increased one hundred–fold because he had an open heaven over himself. In an open heaven God can speak to you more clearly. God opened the heavens over Peter to change his theology.

We only *need* a dramatic encounter when we are called to do something dramatic or have greater impact, like the apostle Paul (he was called Saul at the time) on the road to Damascus. The heavens opened and he saw Jesus (Acts 9:1-9). That happened because he had a great call, and he was about to walk through the opposite circumstances to get him and the church ready.

As another example, Heaven opened over Jesus during His baptism:

"When all the people were being baptized, Jesus was baptized too. And as he was praying, heaven was opened and the Holy Spirit descended on him in bodily form like a dove. And a voice came from heaven: 'You are my Son, whom I love; with you I am well pleased.'" Luke 3:21–22

There are places on Earth where you might feel or hear from Heaven more than others. Ever wonder why Jesus went up to pray on the Mount of Olives? It was an open heaven.

God told Elijah to go to Mount Horeb, and He would speak to him *there,* (1 Kings 19). Moses went up on Mount Sinai to hear God clearly when receiving the Ten Commandments ... twice (Exodus 19; Exodus 24)!

There are places on Earth that have more open spiritual atmospheres than others. Heaven opened for me at Prayer Mountain in Seoul, Korea. I lived in Moravian Falls, North Carolina, for a season, and radically heard God speak over and over. I have also had many encounters in Redding, California. Every time I go to Apopka, Florida, something happens to me. I have had more angelic encounters in Santa Maria, California, than any other place on Earth.

Now, those are places with an open heaven. You do not have to go to these places, because what is open for me may feel closed for you, and vice versa. There are some places that feel more closed off for some, like Sedona, Arizona, and San Francisco, California. But not for David Herzog or me; David Herzog lives in Sedona and encounters God just fine. I lived in San Francisco and started my ministry there, and it still does not feel closed off when I go back there.

But places with Ivy League colleges like Harvard, which draw a lot of intellectual people, feel more closed to me. If your calling is different in nature than mine, you may not feel the same way. Some people have trouble focusing in these places, and others do just fine.

What you want to do is identify a place where you hear God clearly and can open the heavens over yourself. You do not necessarily have to go somewhere. Once you understand how God speaks and how the Kingdom operates, you can actually live under an open heaven wherever you go.

What Closes the Heavens?

A mistake people can make that often closes the heavens off is focusing more on their sins than on God. In trying to become sinless, they are constantly focusing on what is wrong. That will actually get you into a place where that is all you will see, and the heavens get closed off over you.

What are some other things that will close off the heavens over you? Not loving people. Speaking against others, judging and cursing them instead of blessing them, will do it, too. Grumbling and complaining will close the heavens **big time**. In fact, that is probably the biggest thing that will actually close the heavens over you.

Opening the Heavens over Your Life

One of the best things you can do to start opening the heavens over you is to stop grumbling and complaining. Really. Grumbling and complaining can cloud the heavens big time. Fast from negative talk and negative thoughts. Stop listening to negative talk radio or reports on the Internet. Stop this stuff.

Start looking for ways to bless people and see the positive things in them. I am telling you, this has to happen. We are shut down right now in the United States. I believe we have lost our ability to pray and receive answers to our prayers because of our judgments against people in politics. We need to step out of that and step into the Kingdom right now or we will miss what God is saying to us. I cannot stress this enough.

You can change the spiritual atmosphere around you by what you sow and reap every day. If you are sowing complaining, if you are sowing grumbling, that is all you are going to reap.

If you find yourself complaining, then start finding a way to bless two or three times more than you complain. You know, look for good things. It is not just money. Give genuine compliments and say something encouraging. Leave bigger tips. Give some of your time to help somebody. I really want to encourage you to sow into others and be a blessing. This is the secret to an open heaven.

CHAPTER 9

LEARNING WHEN IT IS SAFE TO LISTEN

Counterfeit vs. Real

The counterfeit and the real often match or mirror one another. Even as you are reading this book, be aware that the enemy might try to counterfeit what we are discussing.

God is supernatural and the Creator of all these things. For example, God created transportations, which is what happened to Philip when he was taken from one place to another in Acts 8. God does this by the Holy Spirit, but the enemy has come in with a counterfeit called astral projection, a New Age practice done through a demonic spirit guide.

The difference with astral projection is you actually have the spirit guide take you there. With transportation, the Holy Spirit just does it. You cannot really make it happen. You can ask God, but believe me, I stopped asking and started waiting.

When I stopped trying to make things happen, things started happening more. Just ask God to use you, and trust Him to decide how He will do it.

There are both angels and demons, so prophetic words can be counterfeited by psychic words. The key is to trust God and learn to discern between good and evil. Remember, some encounters can be more dramatic than others. It does not make them any better.

I had a parchment paper appear in mid-air and then vanish into the ground. I woke up with an angel—appearing as a literal man—standing at the foot of my bed surrounded by golden light. Once, I was taken in the spirit to a place I was about to speak at the next day. When I arrived in Bakersfield, California, everything was the same way as I had seen it in the experience the day before.

Again, there are supernatural encounters but God also speaks through the still, small voice. They are really not any different.

We need to say, "God, thank you for speaking," whether that is in a big, dramatic way or quietly in our spirit. I hear God through the still, small voice as much, if not more, than through dramatic encounters. Sometimes with dramatic encounters comes more warfare, which you do not necessarily want.

Supernatural Encounters in the Bible

- Being *transported from one place on Earth to another*, like Philip or Elijah (Acts 8, 2 Kings 2). They were actually taken there. People can experience this by their spirits or by their bodies.

- Being *translated into Heaven*, like Isaiah in Isaiah 6. The apostle Paul was also taken into Heaven: *"I know a man in Christ who fourteen years ago was caught up to the third heaven. Whether it was in the body or out of the body I do not know—God knows"* (2 Corinthians 12:2). I believe by saying *"I know a man,"* Paul was talking about himself and remaining humble. But notice how he did not know if it was in the spirit or in the natural. The book of Revelation is full of these *translated into Heaven* encounters as well.

- Having an *angelic encounter on Earth*. In Acts 12:7, *"Suddenly an angel of the Lord appeared ..."* to Peter and right then and there freed him from prison. There were actual things that happened in the natural as a result of the angelic presence.

- *Spiritual encounters through dreams and visions* (Acts 16:9, Matthew 2:19–22, Matthew 27:19). We can have encounters through these kinds of dreams and visions. They are greater and different than regular dreams.

- *A visitation from Jesus.* In Acts 23:11, Jesus appeared to Paul and told him to go to Rome. If you read Acts 20-23, you will see that previously Paul sensed the Spirit saying something, then an angel stood in front of him, then Jesus appeared to him and it was all confirmed by the prophet Agabus (Acts 21:10–11). Look at the process the apostle Paul went through before going to Rome and into imprisonment. It was a high calling, so it required greater confirmations.

Four Levels of Encounters

There are some misunderstandings today about encounters, so I want to talk about four levels of encounters to help you understand them better. Remember, this is just a generalization.

1. **Level One:** Common, low-intensity types of experiences like subtle impressions or feelings, pictures in your mind, maybe dreams; average, everyday things.

2. **Level Two:** These are more open visions as opposed to the impressions and mind's eye pictures in level one. They might be like Paul's experiences or like Peter's, when he fell into a trance in Acts 10. A dream involving the Lord or an angel would be

level two as well. You can place more weight on these.

3. **Level Three:** Included in level three are angelic visitations or encounters, supernatural occurrences like a transportation or when something else dramatic happens. I had a level three encounter where the wind spoke to me, but it was the Spirit of the Lord speaking through the wind. That was a dramatic encounter and a great example of the kind of depth I am talking about in level three.

4. **Level Four:** Events like visiting places in Heaven happen in a level four experience with God. We know that Jesus said in John 14:2, *"In My Father's house are many mansions"* (NKJV) or *"... many rooms"* (NIV). There are different places in Heaven; it is not all the throne room. Another example: hearing the audible voice of God, but I have never heard the audible voice of God. I have heard a near-audible voice. A visitation from Jesus on Earth is level four as well. I have had one of those. I have also been taken into the throne room of Heaven.

Now, listen to me. There are misunderstandings about encounters. I have heard someone say, "something happened during worship." Afterwards, they got up and shared, "I was taken into Heaven, I saw all the angels, and the Lord wants to encourage you." Do you know what? That probably was a vision or an impression. That was probably an impression of being taken into Heaven, which is okay, but not a transportation.

It was not a *level four throne room experience* because when you have those you will be messed up for days.

I want to tell you, over in Germany I had an encounter with a watcher angel who came into my room (this would be level three). That experience wrecked me for a couple of days. I am telling you, when the presence of the Lord and the fear of the Lord came on me, it was the kind of encounter that really shook me up.

It does not make you any less spiritual if you do not have level three or four encounters. Just know there are these types of things, and they can happen.

CHAPTER 10

MY HISTORY OF SUPERNATURAL ENCOUNTERS

I have had many supernatural experiences and encounters with the Lord—such as decrees from Heaven and the Lord speaking to me about things to come. I have also seen a literal parchment of paper appear before me and it came down, then disappeared and vanished into the ground. I have had the Lord speak to my spirit—not audibly. He spoke to my spirit and said, "I have made decrees. I am decreeing things over you right now."

These things were not just for me. I was living this out for others. If you would like to read more about it, there is a post on my blog called *Decrees from Heaven*. When God gives me these words and experiences, He sometimes asks me to share them and speak it out through Internet based platforms such as my blog, social media posts or my Spirit Connection webcast and/or podcast.

"You will also declare a thing, and it will be established for you; so light will shine on your ways." Job 22:28 NKJV

I needed to share it with others, because that was part of why He told it to me.

Well, if God decrees a thing—wow—it shall be done!

Now, I had that dramatic encounter, but first I had to walk through the opposite circumstance of not encountering God at all. A lot of times this is part of the process. I walk through the opposite and get to figure out how to hear what God is saying.

The Courtroom of Heaven

My first experience with the *Courtroom of Heaven* was in a dream where I had a grievance against someone. Oh my goodness. It was definitely a dramatic dream of a level two or three encounter.

The Courtroom of Heaven was jam-packed in this encounter. An angel met me at the door and I said, "My goodness, this place is packed."

"Yes, we are busy," the angel replied. "We are overwhelmed because of all the accusations that Christians are bringing against each other. It is jamming up the Courtroom of Heaven. Heavenly resources are being taken away from the harvest."

I realized that every time an accusation is made against someone, there are things that get released in the heavenly realm. There are resources that go towards answering prayers. There is a defense that has to happen. It is just like a courtroom on Earth.

The angel went on to ask me, "Would you like to mediate?" and I said, "Absolutely." I know this may sound strange written out here on Earth.

A few days later, I had a dream and found myself back in the Courtroom of Heaven, this time sitting with a mediating angel and the person I had a grievance with. There was a legitimate grievance, but I did not go before the Judge and *settled outside of court*, so to speak.

In the natural, I never contacted the person I had the grievance with; I just had those spiritual experiences. Within a few weeks, I got a resolution without having to say anything.

The Courtroom of Heaven really does exist. I go there to plead cases over people. I have been taken into Heaven through dreams and various spiritual experiences, but I cannot actually make myself go. This is just how it works for me.

In Part Two of this book, *Encountering Heaven*, I will go into a lot more detail about what I have learned about the Courtroom of Heaven.

The Golden Angel

In another encounter back in 2010, I woke up and a golden angel was literally standing at the foot of my bed. It came right after I had given around five hundred prophetic words to people in Apopka, Florida. I came home that night exhausted and went to sleep.

The principle for me in this case was from the gospel of Luke, and I am paraphrasing here, *"The more you sow, the more you reap,"* or *"The more you give, the more you receive"* (Luke 6:38).

I needed revelation about my situation at the time, and I had prayed and released encouragement and revelation to others freely in that meeting. After the angel woke me up, I was so tired I said, "Can you give it to me in a dream?" I cannot believe I said that! I hit the pillow, and went to sleep.

The golden angel was then in my dream and took me to four places that really existed. The next day, I went to those very four places. That was a dramatic encounter because I was about to walk through the opposite situation; that was right before I got sick.

We had a lot of difficult stuff happen, such as accusations levied against me. But that is how I got my mantle of love and compassion—it came after walking through that Job season. But the encounter with the angel helped prepare me.

Another Angelic Encounter: A Writing Angel

One time in 2004, I was sleeping soundly. I woke up realizing that I had an angel hovering over me, whispering into my ear and giving me revelation. I woke up, literally saw it and screamed!

It went away, but the revelation was imparted to my spirit. The revelation was meant to equip others and later became the basis for one of my books.

A Supernatural Transportation

In this encounter, I was transported to Bakersfield, California, where I was going to be speaking the next day. I went to bed as usual. I was taken in a dream to Bakersfield, and was shown the building and new hairstyles of the leaders that would be at the event. They got new haircuts. I was also shown the building. The next day I got there and everything was true. They had their hair done and the building was the same as in the dream.

The key message God had for them came through a vision within that dream. God was giving lights to the *torchbearers* or leaders at the church. It was so important that I was literally transported there to receive this revelation for them. Now, this does not make me any better and it actually happened before I shifted into the office of prophet.

Waiting on God's Timing

Because this is ministry school level material that I am releasing to you in this book, I am going to tell you about an encounter that I do not usually talk about in public. Between 2010 and 2011, right around Rosh Hashanah and Yom Kippur, an angel came into my room and read a decree over me. It told me that I was greatly loved in Heaven and that I was called into this season.

Let me emphasize again that I moved into the prophetic office after twenty years of moving in the prophetic and having a prophetic ministry. Do not try to make yourself into a prophet. You must wait for the Lord.

I was not calling myself a prophet prior to that because if you are calling yourself a prophet and you are trying to get people to believe you are one—they probably will not believe you. And if you are not really called to it, then you are going to be in for a rough time.

That being said, if you really are a prophet, then God is going to make it obvious. With me, my prophetic words make it obvious.

I always just called myself a prophetic person. That is just my thing. Whether you are called or just want to be, do not try to force it. Wait for God to show you, and then wait for Him to promote you.

His timing will be perfect, and the grace will be there too. Just understand that some people are not ready yet. If you are definitely not there yet, it will kill you in the season we are in right now to try and move into an office that you are not called to or ready for. I just want to clarify by *kill* you, I do not mean physically necessarily, but it could cause you a lot of damage and pain spiritually.

My Mom's Angel

I want to talk about my mom's angel that got assigned to me, because I want to activate this over you right now. I was having dinner one night, and the presence of God came into the room. I was by myself, and it was so powerful that I thought it was Jesus. At that moment, I could not even discern. It did not say anything, but it suddenly got close to me.

All I could sense was that it was my mom, who had passed away about twelve years prior. It felt like her spirit came into the room, and my first thought was: "Mom! Does Jesus know you are here?"

I realize that there is some theology that will not let you believe this. How could my dead mother be there? But as far as I knew, this was my mom's spirit. It took me about ten or fifteen minutes to discern, and I heard it speak to me.

It said, "No, I am an angel that was just in your mom's presence in Heaven. I have been assigned to you to bring about the prayers of your mother over your life. I was assigned to her and I am now assigned to you."

Well, I know this: my mom was an evangelist. A short time later, I actually got hold of some letters that were written to my oldest sister, Glenna, who had just passed away. My mom had written to her back in 1984 and in this letter, my mom described an angelic encounter she had and her heart for others, though she did not know that is what it was.

What I remember about that angel is the touch on my shoulder that I felt and the whispering in my right ear. That is how it came to me.

My mom was writing about an encounter she had at a restaurant where she was working one night when she witnessed to a man. She said, "I felt a touch on my shoulder and a whisper in my right ear telling me to go and minister to that man."

As I am reading about my mom, at that moment the angel spoke to me and said, "See? That was me." I tell you, I am almost ready to cry right now.

That angel was assigned to my family for a long time, and now it is assigned to me. That came through an encounter that I could not see, but it was confirmed in my mom's writing. Wow!

South African Angelic Encounters

You know, I had a lot of encounters in South Africa in 2009 when I went down to Cape Town. I came back with three angels: love, fire and revelation. After that, my life and my meetings changed significantly.

I had to call Bob Jones while I was down there, and he said I was getting a mantle of compassion and love. Since then, I have walked through the opposite of love and compassion coming against me so I could learn to understand what I carry.

I almost died during that time. When I returned, I had all these angels in my house. The presence was there, but I did not really see them. I could only see these flashes of light out of the corner of my eye. They were gathering angels and they are assigned really for one thing only—outreach. I asked God, "What do I do?" He said, "Put them to work."

I created an assignment. I did not talk to the angels; I just asked God about them. I made up a list of things I needed to get done. The next morning, they were not there. I felt so cold and alone. I asked God, "Wow. Where are all the angels?" He said, "Well, you put them to work." They are not omnipresent like God. They can only be in one place at one time. It was the most dramatic understanding I had received up to that point regarding how angels work.

A Visitation from Jesus

I walked through some really, really rough times between 2008 through 2015. I am finally getting healed from the sickness that came on me during that time. Those years have been some of the roughest seasons of my life.

I got rejected and was banned from speaking in the churches I helped start. I was lied about and my prophetic words were tossed around.

I was still releasing prophetic words on the Internet, but I secretly walked through the most rejection I have ever experienced in my entire life. Even people who know me and love me rejected me, but I never made a public spectacle about it. Then it came.

On my birthday, March 8, 2008, I was told that in five years' time, I was going to be taken into the Courtroom of Heaven by Satan, but I needed to get through it and I was going to be okay. That season lasted five years and five months to the day. Then on August 31, 2013, Jesus came and I knew He was coming; I could feel Him coming.

I was repenting, and I felt the fear of the Lord come into my room and my house. Then Jesus came in and the entire house turned into a prison.

In this vision, I could see that He was on this glass wall on the other side. What I was experiencing was being in a vision state. I do not know if I was there, but it was happening. Jesus was speaking to me in a prison, and He told me that Satan had asked to kill me and execute my ministry, so I was put in prison under house arrest.

In love, God had put me under house arrest because of the things that He had called me to do. He said, "I have come here to set you free." Then some other things happened between me and Him before it was over.

From there I got extremely sick with Lyme disease for two years. He told me I needed to live until I was 55. I turned 55 the next year; that was a year of grace. I thought everything would lift. In fact, I got healed of Lyme disease at Bob Jones' funeral right at that time, two weeks before my birthday. Then it went on for another year and a half, and I recently got healed completely.

I have been in the Courtroom of Heaven since then. There is repayment for people like me and you who have walked through things, who have had injustices happen, who have been spoken against or have had the enemy overplay his hand.

I know the Lord is speaking to me right now about that. Wow! So, Father, I pray that blessing and hope over them concerning these things.

I want to stop now and activate anyone who stopped listening to God or asked God to stop speaking to them because it was too dramatic, or it scared them or it was too much for them.

I ask you, please just repent right now and get back into those things. You can have balance to be able to operate in the gift. You have a high calling. Do not give up. Grab hold of one of those words.

Father, I ask that you would give grace to receive the volume of insight that you want to give to those who were overwhelmed. Give them grace and a fresh start. Amen.

If you want to learn more about activating your prophetic word, I strongly recommend my book, *God Spoke, Now What?* It is about how to walk through these very things because some might be for now, and some might be for later.

The purpose of some words might be to cause you to run after it. It might even look like something totally different. Even if a word you got is now null and void, God can give you another one.

CHAPTER 11

ACTIVATION

As we close out Part 1 of this book, I want to do an activation prayer that will help you get focused for encountering Heaven and the supernatural.

First of all, I break off doubt. I break off fear. I break them off right now in the name of Jesus where people are feeling like they are less than, like they missed it or they messed up. The blood of Jesus covers it all.

Father, I activate right now the new level of faith where we can have faith in You and that the things that are in Heaven will now come on Earth, coming into agreement on Earth as it is in Heaven.

"I pray that the eyes of your heart may be enlightened in order that you may know the hope to which he has called you, the riches of his glorious inheritance in his holy people." Ephesians 1:18

I pray for open eyes. Open our eyes to see the goodness. Open the eyes of our heart to understand the goodness of God, to understand His glory and His grace.

Father, I pray for a visitation of your love first and foremost, a revelation of who You are, that love, that You are for us and not against us. I pray for an activation of eyes to see, ears that hear, noses that smell that even in the spiritual realm we can feel and discern and understand.

Father, I pray that we can push back those powers of darkness that would try to come and bring the bad things and heal the past right now and bring the good.

So I shift the heavens over you right now, in the name of Jesus. This can happen anytime and right now I shift the spiritual atmosphere over you. I just say right now everything come into line over your life for this next season that is coming.

At Rosh Hashanah in September 2015, there was an opening up of something new over us, and we have moved into a time of blessing. Do not listen to negative reports. Rise above them.

I am telling you to rise above judgments. I am telling you to not get caught up into political banter and all of the negativity that is out there. Rise above because the Kingdom of God is above all. He is doing something new right now, and it involves you. He is going to activate your dreams and spiritual encounters.

I pray for transportations, translations. I pray for whatever we are ready for in God. Give us what we are ready for, in Jesus' name. Amen.

I tell you what. I have been doing this for a long time. I get feedback from people. They start dreaming again, they start activating again. There is something about it. For example, the recent breakthrough I had brought massive healing. I have received it and am expecting even more. I am praying for that for you, too.

Here are some next steps you can do:
- Write down your dreams and your experiences.
- Begin to study the experiences that you have.
- Go back and make some notes on it.
- Do some research in the Bible or on the Internet.
- You could take my *Dream Crash Course* or do the *Hearing the Voice of God 365 Activation School.*

Father, we thank You for Your goodness. We thank You that there is a new calling that is happening right now. There is a new calling coming for many people. God, I pray for healing. I pray for blessing right now, in Jesus' name.

PART TWO

ENCOUNTERING HEAVEN

CHAPTER 12

UNDERSTANDING HEAVENLY ENCOUNTERS

Throughout the history of the Church, believers have shared fascinating stories of heavenly encounters. The Bible is filled with the supernatural experiences of ordinary believers like you and me. For example: Hagar, who was forced into exile with her young son only to be visited by an angel in the nick of time; Isaiah, who saw amazing visions of God's throne (Isaiah 6:1–5); Ezekiel, who saw God's glory (Ezekiel 1); and the apostle Paul, who was taken up to the third Heaven.

"And I know that this man—whether in the body or apart from the body I do not know, but God knows—was caught up to paradise and heard inexpressible things, things that no one is permitted to tell." 2 Corinthians 12:3–4

These encounters are not limited to the Old or the New Testament, and they are not limited to the early Church! I know that you have probably heard modern stories of heavenly encounters, and you have questions. Maybe you have had these experiences yourself.

I encourage you to keep searching these things out for yourself in the spirit of Ephesians 1:17–19:

"I keep asking that the God of our Lord Jesus Christ, the glorious Father, may give you the Spirit of wisdom and revelation, so that you may know him better.

"I pray that the eyes of your heart may be enlightened in order that you may know the hope to which he has called you, the riches of his glorious inheritance in his holy people, and his incomparably great power for us who believe."

In this section, I will be sharing what I have learned about:

- Understanding the Kingdom of God
- Interacting with Heaven
- Courtrooms of Heaven
- Books of Heaven
- Rooms of Heaven
- Counsel of Heaven
- Creating an open heaven over you
- Heaven coming to Earth

Before we start, let's pray:

God, we thank You so much for Your presence in our lives. Thank you for the many people who tell me how they get breakthroughs from our books, articles and online events. Father, I pray for everyone who is reading this with an open heart right now and those who will read this book in the days to come. We pray that You would open the heavens and open us up to hearing Your voice. In Jesus' name we pray.

Getting Started

No two people's experience with the supernatural is exactly the same. You may be just starting out and eager to learn. Maybe you have experiences regularly in some form. Or maybe you used to have experiences, but now you feel blocked.

Recently, I learned that most people either sometimes or regularly experience the supernatural. A smaller percentage of people have yet to experience the supernatural in their lives. If this is you, please do not feel bad. The same goes for those who used to have experiences, but may feel blocked for some reason. You are not left out.

Did you know that the veil between Heaven and Earth is opening up more and more? God is preparing us for some amazing times of global revival. Are you sensing that God is releasing prophetic mysteries? Progressive revelation is happening as God opens up mysteries that were previously sealed because they are needed in this season.

"I have become its servant by the commission God gave me to present to you the word of God in its fullness—the mystery that has been kept hidden for ages and generations, but is now disclosed to the Lord's people." Colossians 1:25–26

We are in a season right now when our lives on Earth will change radically as we grow in our understanding of what Jesus meant when He said, *"on earth as it is in heaven."*

"This, then, is how you should pray: 'Our Father in heaven, hallowed be your name, your kingdom come, your will be done, on earth as it is in heaven.'" Matthew 6:9–10

Purpose of Encounters

Allow me to lay a foundation so you do not think that we are getting our focus off Jesus and the Kingdom. My heart is not that you get wowed by all these things, and feel *less than* or left out if you do not have these encounters. I want you to know that people who have heavenly encounters are not more loved or more favored in Heaven; not at all. As I said, we lay this all on the foundation of Ephesians 1:17 where the apostle Paul said, *"I keep asking that the God of our Lord Jesus Christ, the glorious Father, may give you the spirit of wisdom and revelation, so that you may know him better."*

This is all about knowing God better. When we get to Heaven, we will not be evaluated and judged by our gifts, callings or experiences.

It will be on our love and character. Just keep that in mind. Again, please do not feel bad if you are not currently having these experiences.

"And God raised us up with Christ and seated us with him in the heavenly realms in Christ Jesus, in order that in the coming ages he might show the incomparable riches of his grace, expressed in his kindness to us in Christ Jesus." Ephesians 2:6–7

The apostle Paul said that God raised us up with Christ and seated us with Him in the heavenly realms in Christ Jesus. Listen, you are already interacting with Heaven whether you realize it or not.

"Since, then, you have been raised with Christ, set your hearts on the things above, where Christ is, seated at the right hand of God. Set your minds on things above, not on earthly things." Colossians 3:1–2

You see, Paul was saying this to get you into a heavenly mode. This is not talking about later on in your life—this is now.

Misunderstandings about Heaven

There are some misunderstandings that we need to clear up about Heaven. It is not just a place you go to when you die. There are movies or documentaries you may have seen about people seeing lights or a tunnel you go through to get there. It is a place like that, but it is way more than that.

God dwells there. Angels are there. The Holy Spirit brings things from Heaven to Earth. It is interacting with us all the time, physically and spiritually. It is interactive for us physically and spiritually all the time. We were created to live a life daily connected to God who is in Heaven.

That is why we have a body, a soul and a spirit. We connect to Heaven through our spirit. Whether we are aware of it or not, our spirits right now are interacting with Heaven. Sometimes we will get a glimpse of it. You may have dreams that have to do with Heaven. It is more common than we may think!

Levels of Interaction

There are different levels of interaction. I want to be clear because it is important to understand that the intensity of an interaction with Heaven might vary based on your level of maturity or even your gifting.

- Maybe in the past you have had a general sense or an impression of something that just happened, or something that God spoke to you.

- You could have a *divine coincidence.* I love those. I call them, *God incidences* and these open things up for you all the time.

- Many people have had dreams or visions. In fact, most people are experiencing God through the dream and vision realm.

- There are angelic encounters like the one described in Acts 8.

- There are visitations; a *visitation* is simply when something from Heaven comes to Earth. That could be an angel. It could be Jesus.

- It can be when a message from the Holy Spirit is delivered by an angel of God.

- Your spirit can also be taken into Heaven.

Now, I do not go in my body into Heaven, but my spirit goes into Heaven on a regular basis. This was not always the case though; this has just been something God has done in recent years. As of the time I am writing this book, I have spent twenty–five years in prophetic ministry, evangelism, pastoring, interacting with God and developing my prophetic gifts. We are moving into a season and a time right now where this is happening more and more.

Why We All Do Not See or Hear Spiritually

For many people, struggling to see or hear spiritually comes down to unbelief and doubt, or simply not being trained how to do so. Cessationism emerged about 100 years ago, and claimed that spiritual gifts passed away with the original apostles. You will see plenty of things out on the Internet telling us why we cannot experience God.

Why are so many Christians willing to give up this part of our spiritual inheritance? Maybe you believe, but you just have not been trained in it. Or maybe you have had bad or outdated theology. God is doing something new right now, and has been for the last several years.

Maybe you have judgments against others that have closed the heavens, or it could be your level of maturity. It could be that you are just starting out. Maybe you are advancing, and it is about to emerge for you.

It also may be that you are wired and gifted differently. God speaks to us in these different ways, and a teacher might experience something different than a seer. I try to take that into consideration in all my trainings.

Rooms in Heaven

Did you know that there are rooms in Heaven?

"Do not let your hearts be troubled. You believe in God; believe also in me. **My Father's house has many rooms; if that were not so, would I have told you that I am going there to prepare a place for you?** *And if I go and prepare a place for you, I will come back and take you to be with me that you also may be where I am. You know the way to the place where I am going."* John 14:1–4

This is what is really important for you to understand. Most people think that this verse is talking about when you die. But Jesus is not talking about Heaven being a place in the future. He is saying that He will return to our lives on Earth and open the door to experience Heaven now. The second coming is not just the second coming of Christ mentioned in Revelation 19. It is also that He comes again in our lives. He will come and take us to the heavenly rooms and places He has already prepared for us.

Keep in mind that you do not have to have heavenly encounters to experience God or get revelation. The experiences of the modern–day prophets and seers, such as myself and others, tend to set a high bar. But we can all have experiences with Him at various levels, right where we are at. There is tremendous value in simply hearing God. What matters is to let Christ dwell in your heart.

My calling is to help make things simple for all Christians. I like to release and explain how I experience these things so you understand. I also do that with my prophetic words.

We Can Live in Heaven Now

*"These are **a shadow of the things that were to come**; the reality, however, is found in Christ."* Colossians 2:17

What does it look like for us to live a life connected to God? We are a shadow of Heaven now. There is a lot of teaching on the types and shadows of the Jewish feasts and the temple. The symbolism throughout the Old Testament is meant to show glimpses of God's Kingdom on Earth. It shows how we are often living out these things right now as a shadow of what is happening in Heaven. That is where we take on the characteristics, attributes and even the fragrance of Heaven.

It is not about the rules. I am going to address that belief right now. I want to debunk this thing. The reason that we have gotten off-track is because most of the time people have taken on the rules and not the attributes of God. I am going to address that more as we delve into the next chapter.

CHAPTER 13

UNDERSTANDING THE KINGDOM OF GOD

It is important to understand that the Kingdom of God is more than a final resting place. Heaven is in the future, and it is also now according to Matthew 6:10. We need to bring the heavenly qualities into our lives, *"on earth as it is in heaven."*

Some of the old theology we were taught is based more on getting your *ticket to Heaven* rather than *living under an open heaven* or allowing those heavenly qualities to change our lives so that we go out and help other people. I hope you can hear that.

The Gospel of the Kingdom vs. Grace

Let's do a really quick review of the gospel of the Kingdom versus the gospel of grace, and how it all started.

"In those days John the Baptist came, preaching in the wilderness of Judea and saying, 'Repent, for the kingdom of heaven has come near.'" Matthew 3:1–2

In Matthew 3:2, John the Baptist began proclaiming the gospel of the Kingdom for repentance; Jesus reiterated that message in Matthew 4:17.

"From that time on Jesus began to preach, 'Repent, for the kingdom of heaven has come near.'" Matthew 4:17

It was still based on works because Jesus had not yet been crucified. The audience for Matthew 3:2 and Matthew 4:17 was Jewish people.

Just so you understand, when you read your Bible, and when you read the gospels in particular, the primary audience was the Jewish people because Jesus' message was to Jews first (Matthew 15:24). Though they were still rule-based and under the Law, Jesus began introducing grace. Later, the apostle Paul clarifies the gospel of grace based on faith and receiving. This was important because his audience was non-Jews (or Gentiles), who also needed freedom and grace with God. That is where we are today.

*"However, I consider my life worth nothing to me; my only aim is to finish the race and complete the task the Lord Jesus has given me—the task of testifying to **the good news of God's grace.**"* Acts 20:24

Unfortunately, over the last few decades or so we have gotten back to a gospel of rules, and we need to grab hold of the gospel of grace once again. The gospel of the

Kingdom of God (or Kingdom of Heaven), is a place we go in the future, but it is also an atmosphere that we bring on Earth.

"Once, on being asked by the Pharisees when the kingdom of God would come, Jesus replied, 'The coming of the kingdom of God is not something that can be observed, nor will people say, 'Here it is,' or 'There it is,' because the kingdom of God is in your midst.'" Luke 17:20–21

The King James Version of that verse says *"... behold, the kingdom of God is **within** you."* The Kingdom of God is both **around us** and **in us**.

Jesus had been teaching this for a long time, but somewhere along the way we let go of the understanding that we can change the spiritual atmosphere around and inside us by understanding *"on earth as it is in heaven."*

The Kingdom of God is like an atmosphere—a spiritual atmosphere, more specifically. And biblical principles can bring us into alignment with the Kingdom and Heaven's atmosphere. That is why Jesus told parables about Heaven— to help us understand those principles in earthly terms so that we could grasp them. Did you know there are twelve parables that begin with the phrases *"the Kingdom of Heaven is like ..."* or *"the Kingdom of God is like ...?"*

The Kingdom Is Like

Matthew 13:24	... *a man who sowed good seed in his field.*
Matthew 13:31	... *a mustard seed, which a man took and planted in his field.*
Matthew 13:33	... *yeast that a woman took and mixed ... all through the dough.*
Matthew 13:44	... *treasure hidden in a field.*
Matthew 13:45	... *a merchant looking for fine pearls.*
Matthew 13:47	... *a net that was let down into the lake and caught all kinds of fish.*
Matthew 18:23	... *a king who wanted to settle accounts with his servants.*
Matthew 20:1	... *a landowner who went out early in the morning to hire workers for his vineyard.*
Matthew 22:2	... *a king who prepared a wedding banquet for his son.*
Mark 4:26–27	... *[when] A man scatters seed on the ground. Night and day, ... the seed sprouts and grows, though he does not know how.*
Mark 4:31	... *a mustard seed, which is the smallest of all seeds on earth.*
Luke 13:19	... *a mustard seed, which a man took and planted in his garden.*
Luke 13:21	... *It is like yeast ... mixed ... all through the dough.*

Jesus told parables about what *"the Kingdom of God is like"* to help us understand it in earthly terms so that we can align ourselves with Heaven, create an atmosphere of faith and dispel unbelief.

The Kingdom Is like an Atmosphere

We can create an atmosphere of either faith or unbelief; one opens things up and the other closes off our supernatural connection with God.

That is what I mean by atmosphere. You can have an atmosphere of unbelief that will close things down (Matthew 13:58), or you can have an atmosphere of faith and belief that will open things up for you (Luke 8:51–52).

Many Christians are finding themselves in a closed-down mode. I encourage you to study the parables of Jesus on a regular basis. They are full of insight!

Faith over Works

The Kingdom is more about who you are and who you are becoming as opposed to what you do, or what you have done. Many of us have been so focused on works.

Now, there is a balance to this. There are things that you can do that will align you and help shift the spiritual atmosphere. But you do not want to do it legalistically, especially because legalism has been the root of the problem.

"For the kingdom of God is not a matter of eating and drinking, but of righteousness, peace and joy in the Holy Spirit, because anyone who serves Christ in this way is pleasing to God and receives human approval." Romans 14:17–18

The apostle Paul said the Kingdom of God is not a matter of eating and drinking (by the way, the Jewish rituals at that time were centered on eating and drinking) but of righteousness, peace and joy in the Holy Spirit. See, those are attributes as opposed to rules. If you are not approaching your relationship with God this way already, I want to help you get back to what the Bible says.

We Have to Activate It

We must use the power of believing and having faith to start activating things. Then we can shift the atmosphere to the positive by applying biblical principles such as:

- What you sow is what you reap
- If you give you will receive
- If you believe you will become
- Judge not and you will not be judged
- Humble yourself and you will be lifted up

You have heard these, right? These are biblical principles. They are important because if you begin to sow those principles instead of doubt and grumbling, then they will change you and the spiritual atmosphere will shift around you.

"For as he thinks in his heart, so is he."
Proverbs 23:7a NKJV

Today the focus in Christianity is to get us to pray a prayer of salvation so we can get a ticket to Heaven. That approach used to work when we were living in a Judeo-Christian society, maybe prior to or during the 1950s.

Many who got their ticket to Heaven might discover when they get there that God want them to do a lot more on Earth! What we need is to get Heaven on Earth so that we can change our lives and shift the atmosphere. We will not just be preaching or singing about it; we will be changing the people around us and making disciples as Jesus did.

What Went Wrong?

So, what went wrong with the Kingdom message? Let me just recap it for you. The gospel of salvation was preached over the gospel of the Kingdom. The gospel of the Kingdom is about doing the things that Jesus did and being *out there*, taking risks in order to minister.

Where the gospel of the Kingdom movement went wrong over the last few decades is that we started to value obeying rules over having relationship with God. We also focused on doing what Jesus did primarily inside churches, as opposed to demonstrating it in the real world to people who need God.

Another big mistake has been relying on outdated and irrelevant methods of outreach and evangelism, and neglecting friendship and lifestyle evangelism.

Also, the *Left Behind* book series caused complacency. I am not saying that they intended it to, but it showcased the rapture and the theology that goes with that.

Personally, when I was taught about the rapture, I was taught that you get your ticket to Heaven and then the people who are not raptured and are still on Earth were going to be left to fend for themselves. Well, do you know what? That caused complacency. I do not necessarily think that they intended it that way, but the Church got very complacent with their *ticket to Heaven,* and we stopped caring about the people who were dying around us. Now we have a disconnection and have to do something.

What Is Needed Today?

People today are more open spiritually than you might think. They want to encounter God. Today people will tell you that they are spiritual, but not religious. Why is that? It is because they do not identify with church services or other traditional expressions of Christianity. I still believe in the Church, but we need to find a way to bring God's power in a manner that people will understand.

The next revival is going to be so radical that it will cause division in the Church because the old wineskin will not recognize it.

CHAPTER 14

INTERACTING WITH HEAVEN

Interacting with Heaven is a complicated subject. A number of years ago, when I first sat down at a lunch table between Rick Joyner and the late prophet Bob Jones, I remember thinking to myself, "How do you guys get all those visions anyway? How do you get all that revelation? Do you actually get taken there? Is it like a movie?"

At the time, I was up and coming, growing in the prophetic, and I just wanted to learn. Before I could even say anything out loud, Bob Jones leaned over to me and said, "It is not how it comes to you that matters. It is more important that the Lord is speaking to you."

Of course, Bob did what Jesus did. Jesus actually heard people's thoughts at times. This is not mind reading, by the way. In the occult, Satan will counterfeit things of the Bible. Jesus actually knew their thoughts when He was standing in front of the Pharisees. We can do this through the Holy Spirit.

Here is the deal: what really matters is not so much how the revelation comes to you, but the fact that God is speaking to you.

Seeing Spiritually

"Ears that hear and eyes that see—the Lord has made them both." Proverbs 20:12

We all need eyes that see and ears that hear spiritually. The Laodicean church in Revelation 3:14–22 was lukewarm, which is very similar to where we are today. We are not hot, but not cold. Jesus did not like that, and He advised them to get eye salve.

This is what we need as well so that we can get eyes to see and begin to focus on the supernatural things of God. Then our *spiritual dullness* will quickly begin to sharpen and greater spiritual awareness will come.

Getting eyes to see and ears to hear involves cleaning out doubt and unbelief as well as a critical and judgmental focus.

I say it all the time: being judgmental is what is holding the Church down these days. One of the names of Satan is *"the accuser of our brothers and sisters"* (Revelation 12:10). I mean, why would you want to come into agreement with a name or characteristic of Satan? Jesus was never like that, so we need to clean up our eyes and ears to be able to see spiritually. It does not take a lot.

Connecting with Heaven

There are many ways to connect with Heaven. Prayer and praying in tongues are two great ways. You can also read and study the Bible to understand God's ways and His will. This is so important. You can read the Bible and ask God to speak to you. But you can also read it just to understand Him better.

I remember Jack Hayford saying that sometimes you read the Bible to let the Bible read you and other times you read the Bible to study. Then there are times you read the Bible to hear God, and other times you read the Bible to know God. It is so important to understand the will of God.

Having faith is another way to connect with Heaven because it causes you to rise above your current situation. I am talking about believing that God is who He says He is, and that He will do what He said He would do.

Did you know that when you forgive someone it cleanses the spiritual atmosphere? You can feel it sometimes—that feeling of heaviness lifting and hope returning.

This may surprise you, but one of the ways that I connect with Heaven is through journaling. As I read the Bible, I journal. I listen to God, and I journal what I hear. It is not a *Dear Diary* type of journal, believe me. It goes way further than that, and the more you do it, the clearer His will becomes.

"Blessed is the one who listens to me, watching daily at my gates, waiting beside my doors." Proverbs 8:34 ESV

"I will stand at my watch and station myself on the ramparts; I will look to see what he will say to me, and what answer I am to give to this complaint. Then the Lord replied: 'Write down the revelation and make it plain on tablets so that a herald may run with it.'" Habakkuk 2:1–2

I have learned that by tracking His ways in your life through journaling, you can learn to get a times and seasons anointing similar to mine. That is how I can give those daily, weekly, and monthly words. I have learned to discern His voice over time. This is key; it takes time.

Worshipping and music will open up Heaven over you and connect you to God. One thing I do is put on worship music using an app on my phone. Certain types of music and certain worship leaders open things up for me. You may not have a music app on your phone, but use whatever way you can to play worship music. There are no limits because God is limitless, and what you can do through His love and power has no limits as well.

Take Time to Let Heaven Change You

God wants to fill you with His Holy Spirit. This is not a one-time event. Did you know that we need to get filled with the Spirit over and over? Here is one of those disconnections that we have had. Some people think you get filled with the Holy Spirit once. Some people think there has to be an evidence of tongues. Those are old theologies.

People ask, "Do I need to speak in tongues to be filled with the Holy Spirit?" Well I do, but my mom never did and she was the most Spirit-filled person I have ever known. She is in Heaven now, but I knew there was Spirit-filled evidence in her life. Do not get weighed down with old theology. It is great to get filled over and over and over.

If speaking in tongues is not the evidence of the infilling of the Holy Spirit, then what is? One indicator of how God is actually moving in your life is how you treat people behind the wheel of your car. I am not kidding! How you act behind the wheel of your car is evidence of the fruit of the Holy Spirit—or not. How you treat people who do not believe the same things that you believe, and how you behave toward people on the Internet is also evidence of the Holy Spirit in your life.

So, we want to get that new heart and new spirit God talks about:

"I will give you a new heart and put a new spirit in you; I will remove from you your heart of stone and give you a heart of flesh. And I will put my Spirit in you and move you to follow my decrees and be careful to keep my laws." Ezekiel 36:26–27

Listen, God wants to remove that heart of stone. A lot of people have a heart of stone these days, even Christians. That is another thing that has really gotten us off track.

Heavens Opened over Jesus

Heaven opened over Jesus. Did you know that?

"As soon as Jesus was baptized, he went up out of the water. At that moment heaven was opened, and he saw the Spirit of God descending like a dove and alighting on him. And a voice from heaven said, 'This is my Son, whom I love; with him I am well pleased.'" Matthew 3:16–17

Jesus was baptized and the heavens opened. John the Baptist saw a dove come down on Him, and a voice spoke from Heaven. Heaven also opened during the transfiguration of Christ.

"After six days Jesus took with him Peter, James and John the brother of James, and led them up a high mountain by themselves. There he was transfigured before them. His face shone like the sun, and his clothes became as white as the light. Just then there appeared before them Moses and Elijah, talking with Jesus." Matthew 17:1–3

Jesus' face shone like the sun. All of a sudden His glory appeared to Peter, James and John. His clothes became white light and then suddenly Moses and Elijah were there. It was a powerful event. Now that is a radical time. If you are thinking on a scale of one to ten, that is a twenty, you know? Did you know that we can also experience these things now?

Jacob's Ladder

Think about the story of Jacob's ladder. Jacob received revelation about the coming of angels. He had a dream in Genesis 28:

"When he reached a certain place, he stopped for the night because the sun had set. Taking one of the stones there, he put it under his head and lay down to sleep. He had a dream in which he saw a stairway resting on the earth, with its top

reaching to heaven, and the angels of God were ascending and descending on it." Genesis 28:11–12

He dreamed that he saw a stairway resting on Earth and the top reached to Heaven, and the angels of God were ascending and descending, bringing revelation. This is an open heaven. This is the type of interaction that we can have at night whether we remember it or not.

Jesus quotes this story when He gives a prophetic word to Nathanael:

"Jesus said, 'You believe because I told you I saw you under the fig tree. You will see greater things than that.' He then added, 'Very truly I tell you, you will see "heaven open, and the angels of God ascending and descending on" the Son of Man.'" John 1:50–51

This is open to you right now because God wants to do something new in your life.

Angels and the Holy Spirit

I just want to do a real quick overview so that you understand how it works.

"Now an angel of the Lord said to Philip, 'Go south to the road—the desert road—that goes down from Jerusalem to Gaza.' So he started out, and on his way he met an Ethiopian

eunuch, an important official in charge of all the treasury of the Kandake (which means 'queen of the Ethiopians'). This man had gone to Jerusalem to worship, and on his way home was sitting in his chariot reading the Book of Isaiah the prophet. The Spirit told Philip, 'Go to that chariot and stay near it.'" Acts 8:26–29

We looked at this passage previously in Chapter Six. Philip was given instruction by an angel to go down to a certain road that goes from Jerusalem to Gaza, which Philip obeyed. When he arrived, the Holy Spirit told him to go up to the chariot.

You can see from this story they understood that sometimes it is an angel and sometimes it is the Holy Spirit.

Can I say this? It is not just Jesus doing all the spiritual activity, as we can clearly see in the story of Philip and the Ethiopian eunuch. Here is where we have really missed it. People are talking about Jesus all the time. Do not get me wrong; it is amazing what Jesus does. But there is the Father, there is the Son (Jesus), there is the Holy Spirit and there are also angels that interact with us on Earth. They all serve the purposes of the Kingdom, of course. You will want to discern the difference between them.

Sometimes people say to me (or post on the Internet), that Jesus comes to them every day. You may see their prophetic words claiming this. It could be that they are lacking understanding about what they are experiencing. It is most likely an angel or the Holy Spirit.

I am not saying Jesus did not visit, but if He did, it puts a lot more weight on what you are saying. If you say Jesus comes to you every day and you are releasing prophetic words, it could actually be an angel or the Holy Spirit who is coming to you. I am just saying that we need to learn to discern.

Supernatural Experiences

"When they came up out of the water, the Spirit of the Lord suddenly took Philip away, and the eunuch did not see him again, but went on his way rejoicing. Philip, however, appeared at Azotus and traveled about, preaching the gospel in all the towns until he reached Caesarea." Acts 8:39–40

Look at all the supernatural things that happen in this story with Philip. The eunuch understood the Bible with Philip's help, which was an evangelistic outreach encounter.

When Philip came up out of the water from baptizing the eunuch, the Spirit of the Lord suddenly took Philip away and he appeared in another city. He did not catch a ride with anyone—he was transported. These are supernatural experiences, and God wants us to have these things as well.

PARTNERING WITH HEAVEN'S LEGAL SYSTEM

Decrees from Heaven

I am going to share a supernatural encounter that happened around 1999. I was just praying like anybody else, the way I had always prayed. I was not anywhere special and just in my house.

Suddenly I felt something happen. The presence of God came while I was praying, and I knew it was significant. At the time, I did not yet understand the concept of open heavens.

Afterwards, I went up to take a shower and suddenly in the natural realm the heavens opened in the room. I looked up, and about five feet off the ground an ancient piece of parchment paper appeared. It floated to the floor and disappeared.

I was stunned and I thought, "Wow! What was that?" It just happened so fast. It was kind of bronze-looking and it seemed official. I do not remember what was written on it, but God spoke to me that the prayers that I had just prayed had been heard, and He had issued a decree from Heaven to bring it about.

I did not quite understand, so I emailed two attorney friends of mine and they verified it. They said in a court system a *decree* is something that is issued when a judgment has been made for you. It means that things are now being issued to bring it about.

Courts of Heaven

Before we get deeper into talking about the Courts of Heaven, I want to make sure you understand that there is more than one courtroom. It is not just one single Courtroom of Heaven—there are many different ones. It is similar to how a courthouse has more than one courtroom; the Courts of Heaven also have more than one courtroom.

I want to offer a few more insights regarding the Courtroom of Heaven dream I shared about in Chapter Ten. If you will recall, at that time in real life, I was having a grievance with a publishing company that had violated our contract.

I was having a dream, and suddenly I was taken up in a vision during the dream. It was so brilliant, which is how I could tell the different between the dream and the vision.

I was taken to the Courtroom of Heaven, and it was jam-packed with Christians accusing other Christians. Oh my goodness. Every time a Christian would accuse another Christian, a case would be opened because God is just. However, these judgments we make against one another were plugging up the court systems.

In the dream, I was met by an angel at the gates of the Courts of Heaven. As I took a number, the angel asked me, "Would you consider mediating?" Having a mediator is great because they work towards a win–win outcome. It is not the back–and–forth dynamics of accusation and defense.

The next week I had another dream where I was sitting in the room with the president of the publishing company. The mediator angel was there and we settled the case. Do you remember what happened in real life? I had not even contacted the company, but a settlement came and I got my contract back. It happened on Earth as it did in Heaven.

Remember also, the angel said, "Please tell people to stop accusing each other. Tell Christians to stop." I want to emphasize this because it is unnecessarily taking resources away from revival. It really, really is. Do not take each other to court because I tell you, you are a shadow of things to come. You carry the light. You carry the presence of God.

A legal system in Heaven actually exists. We see a glimpse of this in Job 1:6, where Satan goes into the Courts of Heaven and asks permission to tempt Job. Again in Zechariah 3, Satan stood accusing Joshua the high priest in the Courts of Heaven.

Another example is Satan asking to sift Peter like wheat:

"The Lord said, 'Simon, Simon! Indeed, Satan has asked for you, that he may sift you as wheat.'" Luke 22:31 NKJV

The Greek word used for *has asked* is *exaiteomai*. I am not a scholar, but in a general sense it means *to demand (for trial); to demand or ask that one be given up to one from the power of another,* and when it is negative, it means *to give them up for torture or punishment.* It is assuming a guilty verdict and demanding a harsh sentence. So where it says *"has asked for you,"* it actually means *"demands you be put on trial."*

Courtroom vs. Battlefield

I started having these encounters a long time ago. In 2008, I heard the Lord say that I was being taken into the Courtroom of Heaven. I did not know what had happened, but everything flipped upside down for me. We had a big church split, and I was losing my friends. It was one thing after another.

Then I got a call to go to England to fill in for Larry Randolph at a conference. There was a woman there from Capetown, South Africa, who used to be a judge and is now a prophetess.

There were probably 1,000 people attending, maybe more. When I arrived she said, "You, stand up. The Lord told me that Randolph would not be here, but Addison would." That got my attention! Then she said, "Satan has asked to take your ministry into the Courtroom of Heaven and not only that, he has asked for the death sentence over you."

Now, if you ask a judge for the death sentence and you do not get it, that is one thing. If the enemy has requested the death sentence, then you are about to go through some stuff. She said, "I saw a long line of people accusing you, but I looked up into the Judgment Seat of God and He was not there. You will win this fight if you keep your mouth shut." All I could think was, "Wow." That was the hard part. You know, keeping my mouth shut.

My wife and I and our staff went through an extensive legal battle over my ministry with Satan accusing me. I got banned from speaking in the churches I helped start. I ended up getting sick. I had all kinds of people against me. My prophetic words were taken off of various sites on the Internet. I went through such turmoil from 2008 until 2015. I did have a visitation from Jesus in 2013 to encourage me though.

In 2015, at the end of that period of my life, I was taken into the Court of Heaven with Jesus. Satan was there to accuse me and others, but I was acquitted. When you are acquitted it means you cannot be tried again. It is a very big deal.

Though I have been having these encounters for a long time, I realized the courtroom venue was different than what I had experienced in the past.

I found a book by Robert Henderson titled *Operating in the Courts of Heaven: Granting God Legal Right to Fulfill His Passion and Answer Our Prayers* that describes things that are very close to the experiences I had. Henderson teaches that many people might not be getting answers to prayer because we are using a battlefield strategy as opposed to a courtroom strategy. I recommend reading it.

Now I use this book to teach my staff and other people in my life to pray using a courtroom strategy as opposed to a battlefield strategy. Yes, indeed, we are seeing changes.

As a testimony, one of our staff members had $5,000 stolen by a hacker. She took it to the Courtroom of Heaven, got a verdict, and recovered it all! We were very encouraged with that as confirmation.

Parable of the Unjust Judge

Let's review the parable of the unjust judge for additional insights into Heaven's legal system:

"Then Jesus told his disciples a parable to show them that they should always pray and not give up.

"He said: 'In a certain town there was a judge who neither feared God nor cared what people thought. And there was a widow in that town who kept coming to him with the plea, "Grant me justice against my adversary." For some time he refused. But finally he said to himself, "Even though I don't fear God or care what people think, yet because this widow keeps bothering me, I will see that she gets justice, so that she won't eventually come and attack me!"'

"And the Lord said, 'Listen to what the unjust judge says. ***And will not God bring about justice for his chosen ones, who cry out to him day and night?*** *Will he keep putting them off?* ***I tell you, he will see that they get justice, and quickly.*** *However, when the Son of Man comes, will he find faith on the earth?'"* Luke 18:1–8

In this parable, Jesus is teaching people about prayer. There was an unjust judge and a widow who kept going in and pleading her case day and night.

She kept asking him—over and over and over—to grant her justice. So finally the unjust judge says: "You know, I am going to just grant this and give myself some relief here."

Jesus then contrasts the unjust judge with God, who is a just judge:

"And will not God bring about justice for his chosen ones, who cry out to him day and night? Will he keep putting them off? I tell you, he will see that they get justice, and quickly." Luke 18:7-8a

There are a couple of things to notice in Luke 18. Prayer is like a courtroom and the hidden key is that we need to stick with it and not back down!

"Review the past for me, let us argue the matter together; state the case for your innocence." Isaiah 43:26

Jesus Teaches Us to Pray

Most of us are very familiar with the Lord's Prayer. We tend to speak it to ourselves in a very serious, deep voice: *"Our Father who art in Heaven ..."*

However, there is more to it than just reciting the words. Notice there is a pattern.

"Our Father in heaven, hallowed be your name, your kingdom come, your will be done, on earth as it is in heaven. Give us today our daily bread. And forgive us our debts, as we also have forgiven our debtors. And lead us not into temptation, but deliver us from the evil one." Matthew 6:9–13

Here are some prayer points taken from the Lord's Prayer to help you prepare to pray:

- First, give God praise and worship. That is the *"hallowed be thy name"* part. Thank God for what He has done.

- Ask for the Kingdom to come, because that is the second thing He says: *"Your kingdom come."* Ask God to give you a strategy from Heaven.

- Bring your requests to Him. That is your *"daily bread."*

- Repent, asking forgiveness for your debts as you forgive those who have sinned against you.

- Then ask to have power over Satan.

I tweak it a little bit as God leads, but I use this prayer strategy on a regular basis. But here is the last part I want you to see.

The next set of verses after the Lord's Prayer are:

"For if you forgive other people when they sin against you, your heavenly Father will also forgive you. But if you do not forgive others their sins, your Father will not forgive your sins." Matthew 6:14–15

The point is that forgiveness is the missing piece of getting answers to our prayers.

Making Decrees

"You will also decree a thing, and it will be established for you; and light will shine on your ways." Job 22:28 NASB

We can also make decrees. I use Bible verses to create powerful decrees. You will hear me do this all the time. If you have read my *2016 Prophetic Forecast*, at the end of the book are decrees that I wrote for how to pray these things in and open the heavens over you.

Here is one example from the book:

We decree that we will step into a place this year to have greater authority to see answers to the things we ask for in prayer. *"If you remain in me and my words remain in you, ask whatever you wish, and it will be done for you."* John 15:7

It is easy to breeze over that statement, but you can actually begin to decree that God is going to open the heavens over you.

Steps to Praying More Effectively

I believe that prayer is best done from the heart and not from a model, system or template. But I want to offer some practical tips for praying more effectively.

- Gather Bible verses that have deep meaning for you. I have lists of Bible verses that back up what I need to pray about. Whenever you come across one, put it into a file, a document on your computer or smart phone. Keep it handy and then add to it. I add to mine all the time because this is for battling; these are the weapons of your warfare.

- You can use the Lord's Prayer as a guideline if you would like, or you can be creative with it.

- Write down prophetic promises that God has given to you, especially the ones that you have not seen come to pass yet.

- Be like the widow in Luke 18. Continue to ask. Record your needs, be consistent and record your answers.

- Clear out unforgiveness and judgments. You have to get that piece in there too. If you do this, you are going to see things open up.

My strategy looks like this: I pray various verses based on my needs, and I write decrees from the Bible. The most helpful thing I do is I track it. I am consistent in this. I write down strategies as I hear them and the answers that come. I take communion every day during my prayer time. I do it around 7:00 a.m., but you can do it whenever you want.

I also battle in the Courts of Heaven about that time and you can do this too. You can go before the Throne of Grace with boldness as the apostle Paul said:

"Let us therefore come boldly to the throne of grace, that we may obtain mercy and find grace to help in time of need." Hebrews 4:16 NKJV

That is located in the Courts of Heaven and you can go in there with boldness. To be clear, it is not like I am going into this courtroom somewhere physically. I am going to the same place you have access to. It is the Throne of Grace. It is the Lord we are getting more focused on.

There are places we can go, like the Throne of Grace but there are other places off limits to us. We need to either be invited into those areas or ask God's permission before we enter those areas. I have seven categories I pray over every day, and I track the strategies I see. I end it with communion. It is quite powerful.

CHAPTER 16

BOOKS IN HEAVEN

Books of Life

There are different types of heavenly books. The first one I want to talk about is called the *Book of Life*. We each have a Book of Life, though most people are not aware of this. You will see a lot of the prophets talk about this.

"Your eyes saw my unformed body; all the days ordained for me were written in your book before one of them came to be." Psalm 139:16

The Book of Life over you contains the high calling or destiny that God has for you. It is not guaranteed to happen in your life, though. We need to understand how generational curses affect our calling and destiny.

Our Book of Life has been passed down for fulfillment of a high calling. Generational curses have been assigned to us because the enemy does not want these things to come to pass. So we need to contend for them.

Fulfilling what God has for us is never automatic. We need to get strategies from Heaven. People may receive a prophecy and then sit back and wait for it to come about. Or, they get a verdict and sit back and wait for it to happen. You will need to get in there and battle for it. Many people have missed their higher calling because they did not know how to battle for it. Warfare is difficult, but if you push through it you will be rewarded.

When the prophet Samuel anointed David to be the next king, (1 Samuel 16:13) David became even more successful in battle. He was also an anointed musician, able to drive off tormenting spirits when he played.

Suddenly, things go the opposite way. He is driven from his place of favor, and becomes a fugitive (1 Samuel 19–24). Yes, even after years of being on the run, he did not quit.

Jesus went through the same thing. He was tempted in the wilderness, and got really roughed up at the beginning (Matthew 4:1–11). There were many times when the enemy brutally came against Him, but He still fulfilled His calling.

Peter denied the Lord three times. He went through it over and over, and then God finally changed his theology. You can see the same process with Paul in Acts 9 on the road to Damascus. This is very biblical.

We are looking at people with high callings in the Bible, but there are many others. Some of the disciples are rarely mentioned in the Bible, but they all had callings, too. Pursuing our high calling is like an Indiana Jones movie. Remember when he would go to get the lost treasure? There were always booby traps and spiders and snakes. We have to remove and defeat some similar things.

A traditional belief in Judaism is that once a year our own personal heavenly books are opened and reviewed between Rosh Hashanah and Yom Kippur. During this time, our lives are examined to see if we are ready for spiritual advancement—or promotion—to new levels of maturity. *Rosh Hashanah* is the Jewish New Year *and Yom Kippur* is the Day of Atonement and they fall on different days each year during autumn.

This is from Wikipedia.org

Heavenly Books Opened
According to Jewish tradition, God inscribes each person's fate for the coming year into a book, the Book of Life, on Rosh Hashanah, and waits until Yom Kippur to "seal" the verdict.[1]

I spend a lot of time getting revelation during that season because God is releasing new things.

---

[1] Wikipedia contributors. *Yom Kippur* [2.1 Heavenly Books are Opened] *Wikipedia, The Free Encyclopedia.* Retrieved from https://en.wikipedia.org

"For sin shall no longer be your master, because you are not under the law, but under grace." Romans 6:14

I want to be clear that we are no longer under the law. God still works according to the Jewish calendar though, and some of the feasts can have prophetic meaning for us today. I am not suggesting you get back under the law. You do not have to practice these things, but they *"are a shadow of things ... to come"* (Colossians 2:17).

As an example, on the Day of Atonement a Jewish person spends the day repenting for the sins they committed that year and asking God for forgiveness. We know that we have Jesus, who perfectly atoned for our sins. I just need to clear that up.

"Therefore, my friends, I want you to know that through Jesus the forgiveness of sins is proclaimed to you. Through him everyone who believes is set free from every sin, a justification you were not able to obtain under the law of Moses." Acts 13:38–39

Various Books in Heaven

Another book is the *Lamb's Book of Life,* mentioned in Revelation 21:27. Moses was the first one who mentioned this book and the idea of people's names being blotted out (Exodus 32:32). The *Lamb's Book of Life* contains the names of those who are in Heaven. But do not overthink it and worry about that predestination stuff. If you get hung up on all the details, you will miss the beauty of what God wants to fulfill in your life. Do not allow legalism and competing theologies distract you and take your focus off the heart of God. What really matters is that you press in and pursue what is in your Book of Life.

The *Book of Destinies of Nations* is mentioned in Revelation 10:8–11. I had an encounter about the Book of Destiny that is opened over Persia, which happens to be Iran. God is endless, so there are surely many other books.

It should not surprise you that Satan also has a book against you. It is simply a dark counterfeit, because Satan cannot create anything new. He only copies what is already God's. He was created by God, and he counterfeits the things of God. So whatever God is doing, Satan is going to try to make a legal complaint against it.

Satan came into the heavenly courts to counter the blessing of God in Job's life (Job 1:6) and Joshua the high priest (Zechariah 3). Even Jesus encountered resistance from Satan throughout His ministry. Satan actually came into the Court of Heaven with accusations against Jesus.

"Then I heard a loud voice in heaven say: 'Now have come the salvation and the power and the kingdom of our God, and

the authority of his Messiah. **For the accuser of our brothers and sisters, who accuses them before our God day and night, has been hurled down.*'*** Revelation 12:10

Notice that Satan, who has been accusing you not just once, but constantly, has been thrown down. Even though Satan is there accusing, you have the authority of Jesus the Messiah and the power of God.

"You, dear children, are from God and have overcome them, because **the one who is in you is greater** *than the one who is in the world."* 1 John 4:4

We have power over Satan's accusations, but we have to align our spiritual life and atmosphere in order to grab hold of it.

What Is in Our Books?

Our books in Heaven contain details about our higher calling. They hold our potential and include things that our family and our ancestors were called to do.

We know this about the cloud of witnesses and the acts of faith that were credited to them. People like Abraham were credited for righteousness for the things they believed (Romans 4:19–22).

Hebrews 11 mentions the great faith of many men and women, and that many of them died before what they believed had come to pass. That means that others were born later to pick up those things and complete them.

*"These were all commended for their faith, yet none of them received what had been promised, since God had planned something better for us so that **only together with us** would they be made perfect."* Hebrews 11:39–40

We are all surrounded by a great cloud of witnesses—our ancestors in the faith. So our book also contains things for us to complete that were the callings of many generations.

Even with this amazing invitation, people still feel somewhat hesitant to go for it because of their mistakes, poor judgment and the sins of the past. I want you to understand this—if you ask forgiveness for your sins, they are blotted out. Your sins are not there.

"Blessed is the one whose sin the Lord will never count against them." Romans 4:8

I have seen this over and over. People keep lamenting their sins. They are just so sad. Over and over you are bringing up something to God that He has forgotten!

"Then he adds: 'Their sins and lawless acts I will remember no more.'" Hebrews 10:17

"For as high as the heavens are above the earth, so great is his love for those who fear him; as far as the east is from the west, so far has he removed our transgressions from us." Psalm 103:11–12

"You will again have compassion on us; you will tread our sins underfoot and hurl all our iniquities into the depths of the sea." Micah 7:19

It is essential that you move on from those things, and focus on the positive things God has for you.

How to Interact with Your Calling

Ask God to reveal what your calling is. Look at your generational history to see how Satan has attacked your ancestors, which holds clues to your destiny.

When I walk people through this they say, "Oh no, it is a bunch of garbage. It is rubbish." Do not take that attitude! If Satan is attacking a certain area, what is he trying to conceal from you? What is God's will that is opposite? If there was divorce, then what is God's will over your family? Strong marriages, connection and family.

If there was drug abuse, it most likely has a root in *pharmakeia*, an ancient Greek name for witchcraft. This reveals a high prophetic calling in your family line. If there are witchcraft or New Age practices in your life or your family line, the true call of God is opposite—you have a very high prophetic calling.

A great exercise is to make a list of the attacks in your life, then make a list of the potential opposites. This will help you discover clues. I am not saying that this is the only way to discover your calling, but there are clues if you will look for them.

Take simple, proactive steps regularly to activate the positive, godly gifts in your life. When I first realized that I had a prophetic calling back in 1988, I began going to prophetic conferences and got some training. I read books on the topic and listened to teaching tapes. Activation means adding knowledge (2 Peter 1:5).

Books of Revelation

Books of Revelation are spiritual books or scrolls in Heaven that contain revelation that we need.

Ezekiel 3 is an example of this:

"Then he said to me, 'Son of man, eat this scroll I am giving you and fill your stomach with it.' So I ate it, and it tasted as

*sweet as honey in my mouth. He then said to me: 'Son of man,
go now to the people of Israel and speak my words to them.'"*
Ezekiel 3:3–4

God told the prophet Ezekiel to eat the scroll and
prophesy to the people. That was a book from Heaven.

There are also end time scrolls. Now, let's take a time-
out here on end time theology, because that has gotten us
off track. There is an end time, obviously, but please do not
get off track when you are thinking of this. It is going to
take some new thinking.

*"But you, Daniel, roll up and seal the words of the scroll
until the time of the end. Many will go here and there to
increase knowledge."* Daniel 12:4

Many people are going here and there, trying to predict
when the second coming will happen. It does not matter
what they think, because until God decides to unroll that
scroll, no one will be able to understand it. When the
timing of Revelation and Daniel is revealed, then we will
know. But for right now, nobody knows.

The Books of Revelation and the end times have been
grossly misinterpreted. People have been solely focused on
the rapture, the *"Let's just get out of here"* theory, and the
second coming of Christ. Some even have the mentality of,

"Let's not really do anything because He is going to come back. So that means we can run up our credit cards and spend our inheritance."

God showed me that many people around my age in their 50s and 60s took lots of time off work and spent their inheritances to pay for conferences about the end times.

There was a false word from the enemy that came out in 2007 that sounded real. I heard it myself. It said, "Oh, just spend all your money, spend your time with Me because I am going to do something new in your life and take care of you."

Those who believed that God was saying this ended up bankrupt. They were deceived by the enemy and did not leave an inheritance as the Bible says to do. Then do you know what happened? The next generation, our children, became mad at God. Your children got mad at God if you did that. You fell to the enemy. You did not leave an inheritance as the Bible says to do. I am not trying to make you feel bad. I am just saying that we want to grab hold of God's times and seasons. Listen to Jesus' words:

"But about that day or hour no one knows, not even the angels in heaven, nor the Son, but only the Father." Matthew 24:36

Only the Father knows, and He can decide at any time to delay things.

Books of Times and Seasons

There are books in Heaven on times and seasons. People ask me how I am able to accurately get daily, monthly and yearly prophetic words. They often come through these spiritual books in Heaven. Sometimes I actually read them, but others are just revealed to me when I go into a certain room in Heaven. I am able to access it because I have opened the heaven to it. But there was a cost for me to get it.

What is the cost? Obeying Him in matters of forgiveness and not judging. Being available to God when He speaks. I have to be *on call* all the time. I had to adjust my sleep schedule or I would get no sleep. Right now I am in a season of waking up daily at 4:00 a.m. If I want to be ready to interact with God early the next day, I have to go to bed at 8:00 p.m.

There is a massive amount of warfare that my family, my staff and I go through to do what I do. The suffering and the attack is great, but do you know what? The result and the fruit is amazing.

That said, do not try to put yourself where I am. Do not focus on that. Instead, look at what God is calling you to do.

Treasury Room: Paul Keith Davis

Here is something that I thought was really good about the rooms in Heaven. This is from Paul Keith Davis' book, *Books of Destiny*. He had an experience and saw a treasury room where scrolls and ancient books are kept.

He writes,

> "... I discovered that I was standing in a treasury room of Heaven. Intuitively, I knew that we had been given access to a chamber containing objects of such incredible value that it would be impossible fully to understand their worth. It looked very similar to a great king's treasury vault.

> "... (There) were scrolls, parchments, ancient books, and records. These contained the treasures of wisdom and knowledge hidden in Jesus Christ. It must have been what Paul was envisioning when he penned: 'That is, Christ Himself, in whom are hidden all the treasures of wisdom and knowledge.' Colossians 2:2–3 NASB

"… The large room was filled to capacity with incredible artifacts, including paintings and architectural blueprints, even documents containing the secrets of the universe."

If you have a chance, read Paul Keith's book if you want to understand the Books of Heaven.

Books of Revival

God suddenly began to open the *Books of Revival* to me in January 2016. I have been prophesying about a new move of God for a while now, but the *Books of Revival* are about the times and seasons and how it is going to happen.

I started having major encounters in the Courts of Heaven since then, and my annual prophetic forecast contains the recaps of each year.

CHAPTER 17

ROOMS AND THE COUNSEL OF HEAVEN

Rooms and Departments in Heaven

Keep in mind that Jesus said, *"My Father's house has many rooms."* John 14:2a

I believe our understanding of Heaven has been shaped by stories of our spiritual fathers and mothers who went to the Throne Room (Revelation 4). However, that is not the only room in Heaven. There are the courtrooms, (Zechariah 3 and Job 1), and there are also counsel rooms.

"For who has stood in the counsel of the Lord, and has perceived and heard His word? Who has marked His word and heard it?" Jeremiah 23:18 NKJV

There is your own personal room that Jesus mentioned (John 14:2), and also your family rooms and the Cloud of Witnesses (Hebrews 12:1). These are just a few. There are tons of them.

I was part of a group that looked only to the Throne of Heaven, and I did not even know about these other rooms.

I have never been in the Throne Room, nor do I really want to go. Everybody I know has really had a hard time after they came back. I like to be able to function, so I just receive it by faith. I am not trying to be disrespectful at all or put anybody down. I am just saying that God and Heaven are both very vast and complicated.

Courtroom Reporter

Since 2007, I have been a Courtroom reporter. I started having experiences overhearing the Counsel meetings in Heaven during Rosh Hashanah of that year, when God began to call me into Zechariah 3 Courtroom of Heaven encounters.

In March 2007, on my birthday, I was taken into the Courtroom of Heaven. Then, beginning at Rosh Hashanah in 2007, I went through eight years of testing to get promoted from Courtroom reporter (just hearing) to being invited into the Counsel and Courtroom meetings. I walked through my trial until 2015.

In 2016, I was promoted to being a part of the Counsel of Heaven, and I started having Zechariah 3 Courts and

Counsel of Heaven experiences. I am telling you so that you will get an understanding of how it works.

The Courts and Counsel

Zechariah 3 is important because it helps you understand how Heaven works.

"Then he showed me Joshua the high priest standing before the angel of the Lord, and Satan standing at his right side to accuse him. The Lord said to Satan, 'The Lord rebuke you, Satan! The Lord, who has chosen Jerusalem, rebuke you! Is not this man a burning stick snatched from the fire?'

"Now Joshua was dressed in filthy clothes as he stood before the angel. The angel said to those who were standing before him, 'Take off his filthy clothes.'

"Then he said to Joshua, 'See, I have taken away your sin, and I will put fine garments on you.'

"Then I said, 'Put a clean turban on his head.' So they put a clean turban on his head and clothed him, while the angel of the Lord stood by.

*"The angel of the Lord gave this charge to Joshua: 'This is what the Lord Almighty says: "If you will walk in obedience to me and keep my requirements, **then you will govern my***

house and have charge of my courts, and I will give you a place among these standing here.'" Zechariah 3:1–7

Here we go again. This is the Court of Heaven. Then if you keep reading, Satan is rebuked because he had dirtied Joshua's clothes.

Then the angel of the Lord charged Joshua saying, 'If you will walk in obedience to the Lord, then you will govern His house and have charge of His courts, and God will give you a place here.' This is not a promise for when the guy dies. It is for him now.

Do you see that Joshua the High Priest had a dirty turban and dirty clothes? In other words, Satan had overplayed his hand against him. Could this be you?

Later on, God says if you will walk through the process, *"Then you will govern my house and have charge of my courts, and I will give you a place among these standing here."*

The place God is referring to is with the Lord and His angels and the Counsel of Heaven. So it is possible that you can get into Counsel meetings.

I was a Courtroom reporter. All I would hear was the Counsel meetings. I never really interacted until 2016.

The Purpose

Heavenly encounters can be dramatic, no doubt. At Passover 2016, mine started getting more intense. It did not start off this way, though. It has taken over twenty-five years to get to this point.

I always come back to Ephesians 1:17. Remember it? The point of it all is to know Him better.

"I keep asking that the God of our Lord Jesus Christ, the glorious Father, may give you the Spirit of wisdom and revelation, so that you may know him better." Ephesians 1:17

Reflecting back on many of my encounters, I realize I did not understand them. I can now go back and revisit some of my journal entries from decades ago, and have a much greater understanding of them.

I just want to encourage you that you do not have to go into the Counsel of Heaven. It is just important that you understand they are always going on.

Understanding Counsel Meetings

I have overheard or been part of Counsel meetings through dreams and spiritual experiences, and also just hearing them through the Holy Spirit. I have noticed that there is often a lot of discussion happening, but there is not always a final verdict.

Counsel Meeting for the Next President

There are some prophetic voices that are called to minister and speak to the political mountain. I am not one of them. I am called to arts and entertainment, which is why I stay away from politics.

But in 2015, after the first round of Democratic debates in the United States, I woke up the next morning and heard a Counsel meeting going on. I saw the name of the next President of the United States written on the wall; then it disappeared.

There was a discussion about Donald Trump—that he had a calling to government, but he had fallen to pride. This was a discussion—not a verdict. So, the outcome of the Counsel meeting was to pray that he does not fall to pride. This is all I knew; I did not know who was going to be the next President. I am just offering this as an example of a Counsel meeting.

1969 Repayment Verdict

I woke up one day in June 2016 and heard that there was a verdict to "repay me for 1969." That was the phrase that dropped out of Heaven. I thought, "Where the heck did 1969 pop up from?"

When I went back and looked, I thought, "My goodness." I was ten years old in 1969, and the enemy overplayed his hand against me. It was the year my father was electrocuted and died. I had moved away from my friends, was depressed and wanted to kill myself at that young age.

The Lord had been calling me to something, but my siblings had gotten on drugs back then. There was this huge trauma in my life. There was also an unjust landlord in our lives who made us move, right as I was making new friends and starting to trust people for the first time. We had already moved seventeen times!

But the enemy had overplayed his hand like in Zechariah 3 with Joshua the High Priest. Because I am a burning stick snatched from the flame, you see?

Then in June of 2016, came the verdict from Heaven. This is on my prayer list now, and I go into the Court of Heaven because I had a verdict and I say, "I want to see that. I do not know what it is, but I want repayment for what the enemy did to me and my family."

New Prophets Commissioned

On July 30, 2016, I heard that the prophets were being evaluated for promotion. I woke up at 4:00 a.m. and heard, "Get up." Then at 4:15 a.m., "Get up, because there is news." Sometimes I hear: "Get up, because there is a verdict," but this was not a verdict. I heard, "Get up, because there is some news."

I hear God speak just like you do. It was not audible. I got up and positioned myself. You know, got my morning tea, everything else I needed, and then I heard, "Oh, the meeting yesterday about the prophets being evaluated—today 200 prophets got commissioned." They got commissioned in Heaven. It does not necessarily mean they knew this. Maybe they did. I know that I had an experience of being commissioned in Heaven as a prophet back in 2010.

I gave you these examples from my personal encounters to show you the different kinds of activity that could be heard in Heaven at any given time—prophetic people especially can pick up on these Counsel meetings. However, they may not fully understand that what they are hearing may not be final verdicts. Counsel meetings go on all the time. Sometimes there are verdicts given, but at other times they are simply discussions.

CHAPTER 18

STEPS TO OPEN THE HEAVENS OVER YOU

Secrets of the Kingdom

"The disciples came to him and asked, 'Why do you speak to the people in parables?'

"He replied, **'Because the knowledge of the secrets of the kingdom of heaven has been given to you, but not to them. Whoever has will be given more, and they will have an abundance.** *Whoever does not have, even what they have will be taken from them.'"* Matthew 13:10–12

Jesus told the disciples *'The secrets of the Kingdom of Heaven have been given to you.'* That includes you!

What is He talking about here? Jesus is talking about having the knowledge of the secrets of the Kingdom, which is contained within the parables. This also includes the ability to interpret dreams, and the ability to understand spiritual things.

The condition of the Church and many people today is that whatever we had has actually been taken from us. But the good news is that you can restore what was lost.

You can start by valuing dreams. Start valuing the visions that are in the Bible. Develop your ability to recognize how God is speaking to you through symbolism.

Open Heaven in the Bible

We looked at some aspects of opening heaven over us in Chapter Eight, but I want to go a little deeper here. There are many instances of open heavens in the Bible.

*"In my thirtieth year, in the fourth month on the fifth day, while I was among the exiles by the Kebar River, **the heavens were opened and I saw visions of God**."* Ezekiel 1:1

*"The Lord will **open the heavens**, the storehouse of his bounty, to send rain on your land in season and to bless all the work of your hands. You will lend to many nations but will borrow from none."* Deuteronomy 28:12

*"When all the people were being baptized, Jesus was baptized too. And **as he was praying, heaven was opened** and the Holy Spirit descended on him in bodily form like a dove. And a voice came from heaven: 'You are my Son, whom I love; with you I am well pleased.'"* Luke 3:21–22

"But Stephen, full of the Holy Spirit, looked up to heaven and saw the glory of God, and Jesus standing at the right hand of God. 'Look,' he said, 'I see heaven open and the Son of Man standing at the right hand of God.'" Acts 7:55–56

The Mount of Olives, where Jesus prayed regularly, was also an open heaven. Mount Horeb was an open heaven as well; this is where Elijah went to hear God, (1 Kings 19). There are lots of them throughout the Bible. We need to clear out the spiritual atmosphere over ourselves and create that open heaven with God.

You Can Have an Open Heaven

The point is that you can have an open heaven around you all the time. You do not have to go to a certain place to experience God, (but it is okay to do that if God asks you to).

Once you understand how God speaks and that you can actually begin to open heaven over yourself, you will work more closely with God. Some people believe that only God can do this for you, but that actually is not true.

Yes, He does things for you, but you have to say "Yes." You have to take action. Even receiving Jesus as Lord is a step of action. Faith without works is dead, but works will not get you there alone, so there is a balance.

What Hinders Your Open Heaven?

There are things that will hinder an open heaven. Focusing too much on what is wrong or on sin instead of God's goodness is one. That is what we are living under today, especially in the United States. Grumbling and complaining will also shut an open heaven.

"Do everything without grumbling or arguing, so that you may become blameless and pure, 'children of God without fault in a warped and crooked generation.' Then you will shine among them like stars in the sky." Philippians 2:14–15

But the primary ways we hinder an open heaven over ourselves are judging instead of loving people, speaking against them instead of praying for them, judging and cursing people instead of blessing them.

"Do not judge, and you will not be judged. Do not condemn, and you will not be condemned. Forgive, and you will be forgiven. Give, and it will be given to you. A good measure, pressed down, shaken together and running over, will be poured into your lap. For with the measure you use, it will be measured to you." Luke 6:37–38

Many of us are familiar with verse 38 about giving, but go back a verse and look at it in its context. The whole concept of receiving that level of blessing is based on: *"Do not judge, do not condemn and forgive."*

So if you are not receiving a blessing back from all your giving, you may need to go and clear the spiritual atmosphere.

Clearing Your Spiritual Atmosphere

You have got to get honest before God. I go around helping people and groups do this. We get down on our knees right there and say, *"Lord, show me if I have spoken against anyone ..."*

"Search me, God, and know my heart; test me and know my anxious thoughts. See if there is any offensive way in me, and lead me in the way everlasting." Psalm 139:23–24

"May these words of my mouth and this meditation of my heart be pleasing in your sight, Lord, my Rock and my Redeemer." Psalm 19:14

Get intentional about stopping things that are hindering you. Stop complaining and grumbling; fast from negative thoughts and negative talk. Stop listening to negative talk radio. Stop reading reports on the Internet that are inciting negative things.

Then start looking for ways to bless people. Start looking for the positive things of God instead of the negative—even with our President or other leaders. It does not matter what you agree or disagree with about them, start finding ways to pray and watch God move in their lives.

Did you know that two major world leaders, Pharaoh and Nebuchadnezzar, had dreams from God? Ungodly kings had dreams, and it took a spirit–filled person to come and interpret them. So offset that negativity. I did this back in 2004 and my life has changed.

Be aware of what you do and say on a regular basis. If you find that you need to make a complaint about a truly sub-par experience, make an intentional effort to include two or three positive things as well.

I still complain. Believe me. I use online consumer rating apps and websites. Sometimes I will talk to the manager about a person and say that person should be promoted. This is so important.

Many people are experiencing spiritual paralysis and feel stuck in a *dark night of the soul* or *dark night of the spirit.* This is a condition I call *house arrest*; you cannot get out of where you are, or maybe you have not been released from a past season even though it is dead.

It is time to move into the new!

"I will give you the keys of the kingdom of heaven; whatever you bind on earth will be bound in heaven, and whatever you loose on earth will be loosed in heaven." Matthew 16:19

This ties in to what I am talking about concerning judgments and is so crucial. People, even leaders, are binding you on Earth! This happened to me. A leader said to me, "I do not think you should move forward." I was bound on Earth and suddenly I was bound in Heaven.

Now there are times that we need to honor our leaders. Absolutely. But many people who have been in a *stuck* or paralyzed place might need to get this thing *loosed on Earth* so it can be *loosed in Heaven*. It is time for your calling to get loosed!

I want to declare this right now.

Father, I call forward those who are stuck in the past, those who are under house arrest, those who have been in the dark night of the soul or the dark night of the spirit for too long, and those who need to be released from dead seasons. I now loose you. I loose you on Earth to be able to step in this new season in Heaven, in Jesus' name.

Now watch for this. You might need to take a positive step toward this and see what happens. Go back and read that verse about being bound and loosed, and pray over your own life.

Ask God if you have done this to anyone else. Also, see if you recall anyone with authority who has done it to you. It could even be family members of friends. If this is the case, forgive them, release them and repent of doing it to others. This is so important right now.

CHAPTER 19

HEAVEN IS COMING TO EARTH

As you have read in some of the experiences I have shared, Heaven coming to Earth can be more dramatic sometimes than others. Know that God will only give you what you can handle right now, based on your level of maturity. Remember that greater encounters bring greater warfare. You are not any less if you are not having them, and God may actually be protecting you for now. You can trust Him with this.

Hidden Revelation

"I will give you hidden treasures, riches stored in secret places, so that you may know that I am the Lord, the God of Israel, who summons you by name." Isaiah 45:3

God is positioning and summoning you by name, extending an invitation from the Spirit to one of the greatest moves in history.

I do not have time to go into all the prophetic words about the hidden ones. That might be you. That might be your son or your daughter who used to serve the Lord, or others you know who have a strong call of God on their lives, but they have been hidden away.

So therefore, I call forward the hidden ones who are about to come. God says, "Do not worry, I am about to do something. A trumpet blast in the spirit is going to come, but as it happens, remember Isaiah 43 …"

"Forget the former things; do not dwell on the past. See, I am doing a new thing! Now it springs up; do you not perceive it? I am making a way in the wilderness and streams in the wasteland." Isaiah 43:18–19

God is doing a new thing right now.

New Things from Heaven

As He does a new thing and as this new revival starts, we need new strategies on how to reach people with God's love, and how to get finances to do it.

We need new ministry techniques for the new revival; new music, new sounds, new language, new art, new writing, new creative expressions.

But here is the thing: you cannot develop this with your current thinking or theology. God needs to release you from the past to be able to get in line with Heaven for what He is doing right now.

New Outpouring of the Holy Spirit

*"In the last days, God says, I will pour out my Spirit on all people. Your sons and daughters will prophesy, your young men will see visions, your old men will dream dreams. **Even on my servants, both men and women**, I will pour out my Spirit in those days, and they will prophesy. I will show wonders in the heavens above and signs on the earth below, **blood and fire and billows of smoke. The sun will be turned to darkness and the moon to blood** before the coming of the great and glorious day of the Lord. **And everyone who calls on the name of the Lord will be saved.**" Acts 2:17–21*

God is going to pour out His Spirit on women right now. Over the next year we are going to see women rise up like never before, and this might rattle some theologies.

The whole idea of the second coming happening at the blood moon prophecies back in the fall of 2015 was inspired by this verse about the moon being turned to blood.

Many people thought that was going to be the second coming of Christ. No … it is the second coming **of a revival**

that we need. It is a revival that is going to happen before He comes. So it was misinterpreted.

Here is what is going to happen. *"And everyone who calls on the name of the Lord will be saved"* (Acts 2:21). This means anyone, no matter what political party, no matter what gender or anything else that has disqualified them in the eyes of the Church. God is going to the outcasts, and new doors are going to open in Heaven.

New Heavenly Encounters

On Christmas morning 2015, I woke up seeing an Ezekiel 40 measuring angel. The angel was just measuring and measuring and measuring, and I knew it was for the new revival.

I talked about the new revival to the outcasts in my *2016 Prophetic Forecast* because I saw the Gathering Angels and the Worker Angels arrive. It was an amazing experience. Then everything kicked up.

In January 2016, I saw the Keys of Authority Angels. They did a big shuffle of the keys of authority, gifts and callings. They were taking back these keys of authority that other leaders or prophetic people had not used, or they had become judgmental or they did not know they had them.

In February 2016, I saw Peter's evangelistic net. It had sunk to the bottom of an ocean and it resurfaced. When I saw that, I knew that we have not seen a revival in years—decades even—because of all the craziness going on.

That same month, I saw a giant golden door open at 4:44 p.m., and I knew it was related to Ezekiel 44:4: *"Then the man brought me by way of the north gate to the front of the temple. I looked and saw the glory of the Lord filling the temple of the Lord, and I fell facedown."* That is what is going on. The glory of the Lord is coming back. We are going to see some new things.

In May 2016, I was summoned into the Courtroom of Heaven. I usually take my prayers in about 7:00 a.m. each day, like anyone else would. I heard someone say, "Come back at 8:08 a.m." I had never heard that before.

At 8:08 a.m. I positioned myself by faith and went there in my spirit. Aimee Semple McPherson and Rex Humbard were standing in the Counsel of the Lord. They had assignments. They were there with this stack of papers containing assignments that they were not able to complete. Rex Humbard founded the first Christian TV network back in 1953, the first guy to ever put his church's service on TV for the purposes of outreach. Aimee Semple McPherson was one of the first women to broadcast on

Christian radio stations. So they were giving their assignments out.

In June of 2016, I saw an Ezekiel 34 angel. God said, "Son, prophesy Ezekiel 34." I knew that there were mean shepherds and fat sheep that had driven away these weaker sheep. God wanted to raise up *weak–sheep defenders*. I have done impartations for that.

"You have not strengthened the weak or healed the sick or bound up the injured. You have not brought back the strays or searched for the lost. *You have ruled them harshly and brutally. So they were scattered because there was no shepherd, and when they were scattered they became food for all the wild animals."* Ezekiel 34:4–5

"Therefore this is what the Sovereign Lord says to them: See, I myself will judge between the fat sheep and the lean sheep. Because you shove with flank and shoulder, butting all the weak sheep with your horns **until you have driven them away**, *I will save my flock, and they will no longer be plundered. I will judge between one sheep and another. I will place over them one shepherd, my servant David, and he will tend them; he will tend them and be their shepherd. I the Lord will be their God, and my servant David will be prince among them. I the Lord have spoken."* Ezekiel 34:20–24

"You are my sheep, the sheep of my pasture, and I am your God, declares the Sovereign Lord." Ezekiel 34:31

On July 4, 2016, I woke up hearing, "Rejoice, for the time has come!" over and over for an hour. That was the crossing over. It has nothing to do with the independence of the United States. This has everything to do with the Kingdom of God. God is moving right now for a revival all around the world. When I have shared this message online, the anointing is overpowering.

I want to call this forward in your life right now. This is a prayer of impartation.

God, I pray that You would call us all forward for this season right now. Unleash the people who have been stuck in the past, who have been under house arrest, the hidden ones coming forward right now. I pray in the name of Jesus that there would be an anointing that would touch them today.

God, I pray that right now in the name of Jesus we would have eyes to see and ears to hear as the Spirit says in Revelation 4:1b, "Come up here, and I will show you what must take place after this ..."

So that we can rise above the pollution from the political–religious spirit and above the wounding things that have been happening within Christianity. God is calling you forward into this time. Right now He is calling you, He is calling your children, He is calling people to something new that is so radical it is going to create a civil war in the church. The Lord is calling you forward right now and, God, we say we want Your will. Reveal Your will.

I pray for dreams and visions to be activated. I pray for spiritual experiences. I pray for encounters in Heaven. God, would you open up and rend the heavens and come down and change things? Bring healing. Bring restoration. Bring those things that have been tucked away and pushed aside along with the people who have been pushed aside and I pray in Jesus' name that You would now bring them forward into this season. I activate you.

God is doing group impartations. He is setting people free in massive groups. I was in a meeting in South Carolina, and we saw the heavens open and a revival angel came down that was so powerful. I had not seen anything like it. I pray for that to happen over you, that God would bring that open heaven that you need.

Right now, Father, in Jesus' name, I pray for the final activation. You said that if anyone blesses the work of a prophet you receive the prophet's reward, and I take the names of the people who blessed me and my staff and the work that we are doing in Los Angeles and around the world in activating this new move of God. I bless them right now and I ask that even in the next few days that there would be something that opens up at a greater level for them, in Jesus' name.

Blessings to you, and may you walk under an open heaven and know the Father who loves us all.

PART THREE

QUESTIONS AND ANSWERS

FREQUENTLY ASKED QUESTIONS

In this section of the book, I will be sharing with you a number of questions that came up during recent seminars and my answers to them.

Doug, if you being sick was a living parable of the church being sick, how does that relate to your current recovery and healing being a prophetic sign for the Church? If you are a living parable of the Church, how does your healing relate to the Church now?

I had a dramatic level of healing just recently. Part of the healing was to cleanse the body, and I actually had to cleanse my blood. The biggest part of my healing was through a treatment called UBI which involves running your blood over ultraviolet light. So, it is cleaning the blood. It is symbolic of cleaning our understanding. The light of Jesus is going to cleanse things. Why did I have this stuff come against me? People ask me this a lot. They want to know if it was because of my connection with witchcraft and the occult in the past. Because that is what Henry Wright says; he believes that is the root of multiple chemical sensitivity. I cut all that stuff off. No, it was witchcraft coming against me, actually. God is cleansing the blood right now. He is bringing some new experiences.

Can all believers have all types of encounters, or does it depend on your spiritual gifts?

Well, technically, we can all have all types of encounters because Jesus did, and He was not limited. You will probably operate in one over the other, but you can have them all. It is sometimes called the Holy Spirit tool belt, and you have access to all of it. You will probably operate, maybe, more strongly in one gift or another; maybe through dreams or maybe it is seasonal. You may be a strong teacher, and that is how God speaks to and through you.

If I have been asking God for supernatural encounters, and they have not been happening, is it my fault? Is it sin? What do you think it is?

Well, first ask God. If you have been asking for encounters and it is not happening, it could be seasonal with you if you used to have them. You might need to open some things. I always do this. When I stopped having experiences for a time years ago, I watched a William Branham video. (He was a healing evangelist from the 1940s and 50s.) He said in a video that He was not able to hear the Lord. He said, "the angel would not stand next to [him]." He could not get the word of knowledge for a person, and he said, "Lord, if my tongue has cursed me knowingly or unknowingly, I repent." Then the angel came and it opened up. This is what I do. I say that prayer all the time. "If my tongue has cursed me knowingly or unknowingly, I repent." I believe that judgments really may be one of the things that are holding people back.

How can I increase the frequency of open visions in my life? I am wondering because you said that you see a little bit, and you hear a little bit. How do you get more?

You can have an open vision or an inward vision. An inward vision is something that you do not necessarily see openly. Do you know what? You cannot do anything to increase those. God is the giver of those things. You can ask God to do it. You can open yourself up to it, but God is the giver of those things. I do not really have very many open visions. Every time I have had one it has been a surprise. It looks like a literal picture in front of you or something that is inward, either one.

What you can do is develop the fruit of the Spirit, and seek to know God better. This is what is going to matter. You know, there are times when God is waiting on us, but we need to come into agreement *"on earth as it is in heaven."* Study this for a little while and see what happens to your heart: *"But the fruit of the Spirit is love, joy, peace, patience, kindness, goodness, faithfulness, gentleness, and self-control ..."* Galatians 5:22–23 ESV. That is how you do it. Focus on those things, and ask God to give you more.

I know the heavenly realm is intertwined with the natural realm, so how do I discern if something is from the natural realm, or from the heavenly, or if it is my gift or if it is an angel? How do I know?

That is a good question. That takes journaling and discernment, and having God show you. Go back to the last time that you know God spoke to you, or you felt the presence was there, and study it. Make some bullet point notes. How did it come to you? Listen. Even though it was internal in the Spirit, did it feel like it was coming from the outside-in or from the inside-out? Because the outside-in encounter is probably an angel. The inside-out message is probably the Holy Spirit. Of course the Holy Spirit runs it all, but there could be an angel in the room. You have to take notes, and you have to ask God to show you.

I have heard people say that when they are called into ministry an angel or the Lord will show up. But what happens if that does not happen, and you still feel really called to a ministry?

Another good question! That statement is a little out of balance though, because if you are called into the ministry not everyone gets those encounters. If you have a dramatic calling—you know, a very, very dramatic calling—you might have a visitation, like the apostle Paul did. He had a dramatic calling. Notice though that the Bible does not say anything about Philip having a dramatic encounter with God. In fact, he just served as a deacon. He ended up having some radical things happen to him, but he faithfully served as a deacon. So it is an out of balance message to say that.

This is normally if you are called into an *office*, that is, a high level of responsibility in the Kingdom. Once you get there, it is more common to have an encounter. But if you go by faith, you go into what God has called you to do by faith, and then God will absolutely confirm things to you.

Now, I just want to say this. I was told that Jesus had to come and commission me before I could be a prophet. Do you know what? I was commissioned by an angel in 2010. I had a visitation from Jesus later. My point is there is no formula to it. God is outside of all that, but if you are called into something ... believe me, God will confirm it to you.

There are too many people who are acting like prophets and apostles that are not there yet. Maybe your calling is there, but you are trying to get a title or you are trying to do this. You do not want to get there before you should. You want to be a servant and be humble, and let God lift you up and promote you in due time (1 Peter 5:6).

How does a person stay in the presence of the supernatural when battling their human mind?

I just create a naturally supernatural environment. God created your mind too, right? There are times when it will wander in and out. Yes, you do have to get your soul to quiet down. So, what do I do if the presence of the Lord comes, or when I am doing something, and my natural mind starts doing things?

I pull out a pen or whatever I have handy. I start making notes of what my mind is saying, kind of like a dump document. I dump it all out because my mind might be saying things that I need to dump out and flush from my system. Or if I have the presence of God come on me while I am writing, I will dump all the negative immediately. I will get it out of there so I can get back to the supernatural. You can live in the place of both, but you are still natural. You are still a person. You will have doubts. You still will have these things going back and forth between the two.

Can you go over the difference again between hearing from God and just having a good idea? I am a computer network guy and I get thoughts of inspiration, but how do I know it is not just me? Maybe it is God?

The best thing that you can do is to record those inspired thoughts. Write them down, and test a few of them or ask God to confirm them, especially in your computer network. I was a computer network guy as well, and you tend to think more logically. Ask God to confirm one of your inspired ideas, or take some steps towards one and see what happens. It is often just trial and error or confirmation, stepping out and taking a risk.

I get ideas. I get six ideas an hour to this day. I do not implement them all. I do not know if they are mine or not. Once you start opening the heavens over you, you can move into a place where the Lord is moving through you all the time. But if you are not there yet, and you are still learning, He is training you so you do not want to start to activate every single idea. You will want to grab hold of one thing and try it for a bit, and see how it goes. Try that.

If someone in ministry tells you that you are supposed to do XYZ and great things are going to happen, but you never do XYZ, then what does that mean?

You received a great prophetic word, but it did not happen the way you expected. There could be a number of reasons why you have not yet see the fulfillment of the prophetic word. Maybe you did not activate it. It may not have happened because maybe the timing got thrown off, or because there were other people that were involved. Maybe the season shifted and it just did not happen, or it could be that it is something you are called to that is greater than you understand, and you are going to have to battle through it.

Think about David. David was anointed to be king by Samuel, the same prophet that anointed King Saul. David continued on from his official anointing by Samuel for over ten years with everything looking opposite for him. No matter what the prophecy was, it looked opposite in his life.

It was the same with Joseph. He received dreams from God, but his life all looked opposite for many years. What can happen is that the greater your calling is, the more you will have to battle.

This is why you might not be seeing the word come to pass. The purpose of words like those is so that you will battle for it. I see so many people that rest on their prophetic word and do not do anything to activate it, and then it goes null and void because they either did not step out or they stepped out too soon. You know, just stay in there with it. You probably have a high calling, and you just need to keep on towards it. Keep asking God and then see what happens.

I work sixty hours a week so I do not have much of a life, but what am I supposed to do with all the prophetic input and experiences that I am having? What does God want me to do with it?

Well, that is where you have to look for His timing. Continue to value it. I asked God to stop giving it to me at one point. I want to pray and activate people who have done that because it was overwhelming. That is the last thing you want to do is ask God to stop speaking to you—because He will. He will take it away. I had to *reactivate* it. Keep valuing what God is saying. Ask Him to give you a strategy, especially if you are working 60 hours a week. I released something on Kingdom finances called *Flipping Your Financial Future*, maybe check that out to learn to get strategies from God to free up your time to do what He has called you to do. We really want to get into the things of God. Continue to value them. Keep moving forward.

I had an event that happened a few months ago. I was asleep in the night but awakened by something so strong that I sat up in bed, and I was knocked down. I was filled with electricity and these waves of power kept going through my body, and I kept seeing fire. I felt like I was going to die, but I also felt it was God.

Yes, that is very biblical. That is the presence of the anointing of God. If you look it up, many times when someone has a divine encounter in the Bible, they fell down like a dead man. So, yes, that was for sure God. That was God imparting something to you. These are special moments. God loves you. He wanted to give you something. He wanted to anoint you with something. I get moments all the time, and they come with crying. The presence comes on me, and I go into tears. I do not understand why that is.

I am really passionate about seeing the heavenly realm, really passionate about seeing God. I want to see angels, I want to spend time with Jesus, and that is my whole focus. I am wondering if it is okay to be this passionate?

Of course, it is okay to have passion for it. If you are not seeing it yet, know that it is okay. Do not give up, but if that is causing you to feel *less than,* you will want to move towards being a son or daughter first and foremost.

You know, understand who you are in Christ. But otherwise, absolutely! I have a pursuit. I am so hungry. In fact, that was the biggest complaint people had against me early in my Christian life at my church back in the late '80s and mid '90s. They had this complaint that I was too zealous.

I would go to conferences, always trying to fill my hunger. I always wanted more. That is all I would do—seek to hear God.

Do you know what? It paid off. It all paid off. I know it seems out of balance sometimes, but the hungry get fed. The thirsty get the drink. Keep going after it with all you have, but do not think that you are less if you are not getting it. Do not let the enemy mess with you.

Going back to the idea of accessing the Kingdom realm. Is it okay if we are using our imagination and faith to start seeing in the Spirit and start the flow, or should we be waiting for something just to *fall* on us?

Well, if you are training with the Lord you can do lots of things. I have a training called *Hearing the Voice of God 365*. It is an online activation school. It is twelve sessions, and I walk through some of this learning curve. Some of these ways of hearing God, you want to activate and practice on a daily basis. You can do exercises. For instance, when I train people in the prophetic, I ask them, "If you were to describe this person as an animal, what type of animal would they be? What if they were a movie character?"

You can start doing that to activate your seeing ability. Those are activation training exercises. Yes, you can practice. As far as going into the heavenly realm, I have never done that where I actually imagine and do it, but I will tell you what, when I go to battle against the enemy I sure do go in and battle. I position myself intentionally.

It is the same with worship. You know, this is a principle when we go to worship God. That is why most people take a long time because they have to actually get their body into a certain place in order to connect in worship.

They may clap or they may raise their hands; they have learned what works for them. It is the same thing when they are praying—they position themselves for it.

The second part is your soul. You have to get your mind focused on the Lord, and then the spirit kicks in. So, yes, what you are talking about is very biblical. You know, body, soul and spirit work together to get into the presence of God.

When I lay awake at night I have felt my spirit go places with Him, but I just get impressions of what is happening. Is that biblical?

Yes, it is. Those are impressions. That is where God wants you right now because the greater things come with more warfare.

God wants you in these lower levels right now. These impressions are just as good. I love what Rick Joyner used to say: "Even if ten percent of what is happening to you is God, it is better than nothing."

Rejoice in what you have. It takes time to get your mind trained and your soul trained. It takes time, but what happens is we have *kicked the baby out with the bath water.*

We do not let anyone practice! We are all afraid of using the soul, but remember that it takes time and you will have to activate yourself.

Can the fruit of the Spirit manifest as beings or angels? I saw what looked like three really large fireflies when I was getting ready to pray, and I felt like it was joy?

When you saw those angels, those fireflies, what you felt was joy. That was their purpose. When I see angels I do not really have names for them. I hear functions. In your case their function was to bring joy. There is an angel of love that comes. That is the function of it. So, yes, and the fruit of the Spirit is probably in everything. I would not say that they were the fruit of the Spirit, but rather they brought the fruit of the Spirit. That was their purpose.

I want to walk in God's glory and presence, but I have not been able to for a very long time. I remember when it left me and I want it back, but I do not know what to do.

If this is you, can you take out your journal and start praying and asking God, "What happened during that season? How long did it last? What else was going on in my life?" Sometimes people think that it is because of something they did. It could have been. Or it could be because God is training you for the next level. He will often pull back.

He will give you something, and then allow for a season of hide-and-seek. It is very biblical, actually. Look at what happened with David when Samuel anointed him to be king. God blessed him and then suddenly pulled back, and he had to run because God was developing his character. So it could be that you are going through a testing time. I went through a massive testing time just recently.

I am going to pray to activate this over everyone who used to feel God or used to have encounters, but you do not right now.

So, Father, I pray in Jesus' name that You would activate the spiritual gifts, activate everything that is needed to open up Heaven for those who feel stuck in a previous season. Those who used to get it who do not now. I ask that You would reveal anything that the enemy does not want us to see about the situation, and I push back the powers of darkness that have been trying to stand in the way of people having amazing encounters. Now I pull you into the current season, in Jesus' name.

What is the difference between our spirit being taken to Heaven in a heavenly experience and being seated in heavenly places?

That is a very good question. Yes, being seated in heavenly places is something that we all have. We are in this place—it is one of those mysteries of Christ that Paul was revealing. Being seated in heavenly places is about the authority you have as a believer, but there is the thing that the enemy does not want you to know. He does not want you to know that you are actually a son or a daughter, and that you are actually someone greatly esteemed, that you are the apple of God's eye. The enemy does not want you to know that. Seated in heavenly places means that your spirit is in a place of authority by faith because of what Jesus did, and you come into agreement with that. Being seated is a seat of authority. It is walking in authority.

Now, having heavenly experiences is a bit different because that is maybe interacting with various aspects of Heaven. It could happen in dreams and visions.

Someone told me once that I needed to be prepared to see demons as well as angels if I am allowed to see in the spiritual realm. Is this true?

Well, one of the things that I have noticed, one of the downfalls of the Church that I am going to mention here, is that we have gotten too focused on demons. For instance, if I go into a church and start talking about the presence of angels, the people start getting uncomfortable. But if I talk about a demon being in the room, most of the time there is 100 percent agreement. That is a bad day in the Church. That means that we are demon–focused, and the Bible is not a book about demons.

However, we do not want to be unwise about it, you know. I believe in focusing more on God, but my staff and I are in a season right now where we are going in and cleaning up things. We are going in and going through a John 15 purging time. That is where we actually have to discern some of the demons.

I used to see demons all the time. I came out of the occult back in 1980s. I was tormented. I began to pray and shift from seeing demons to seeing angels. My whole life in ministry changed.

So, the answer is no, you do not have to. In fact, I would encourage you to see angels over demons as much as possible. However, you might have the gift of discerning of spirits, and if you have that you are going to see demons as well.

But I want to encourage you to read or take some of my courses because if you are seeing just the negative without looking for the positive, understand that God wants to help you so that you are not shortchanging that gift. We have to be able to look at the demonic like Jesus did.

He went up to someone and yes, He sometimes identified a demon oppressing them, but He did not stop there. He brought freedom and the presence of God into their life. That piece seems to be missing these days.

Do you always feel the presence of an angel? Someone told me I have one, and I think I do, but I do not feel anything.

Well, we all have angels. Whether you feel it or not, it does not matter. Throughout the whole New Testament, throughout the Bible, angels are interacting all the time. So, every single one of us, yes, has angels.

There are angels that are with you for life (some call them guardian angels) and you are so used to them that you do not sense them. In fact, I want to do an activation right now for people who have not sensed angels, who do not know the difference between the Holy Spirit, an angel, and Jesus.

Father, I ask You to come and activate the ability to learn to discern the difference between the Holy Spirit, Jesus, angels, demons, and all the other Kingdom things that are going on around us. In Jesus' name, I command these things to line up over you. I was seeing the tumblers in a lock, some are suddenly coming into place for many of you. I ask now that we would have eyes to see the angelic around us in Jesus' name.

Now, I will be honest with you. For me, it changes from season to season. When I lived in Santa Maria back in 2009 through 2013 or so, it was the most angelic season I have ever had. I saw literal angels, I saw lights, I saw and sensed them. I do not have that level of sensitivity right now.

I am not in that season or maybe it was the place. I do not know, but now that I am back in Los Angeles, the City of Angels, I actually know that the angels are there. Now things are different and I am having more heavenly encounters than the previous season.

Are there places that are open portals to Heaven where you can hear or see better when you are there?

Yes, there are places. By the way, as a way to understand portals, review Revelation 4:1, where John gets this revelation. I have been talking about this a lot in my prophetic words. An angel comes and says, *"Come up here and I am going to show you the things that will be coming in the future,"* but it was a door that appeared. A door appeared in the spirit and he said, *Come up here.* If you look up the Greek word *thura*, it means door and it also means a portal or access. This is throughout the Bible. It is not a New Age thing. There are some that are closed off, but there are many open places too.

Why would Jesus go up on the Mount of Olives to pray? Why did Elijah go to Mount Horeb? Why did Moses go up on Mount Sinai? You know, there are places where we can feel more connected. You can open a heaven over yourself.

If you have ever been around someone where you can feel the presence of God, that is because they walk under an open heaven. It does not happen automatically.

I got filled with the Holy Spirit in San Francisco in 1998, and I found that there were lots of places that felt closed off. But then I could go and pray in certain places and feel the presence of God. In fact, there was a prayer mountain in Belmont, California, with a training center on it at that time. Later, God showed me how to open the heaven over my secular job in San Francisco. Then, when I developed my computer business, God trained me to do prophetic evangelism by going into peoples' cubicles at work in San Francisco and being able to prophesy into people. I would actually operate under an open heaven, but I did not realize at the time what I was doing.

Are there any protocols that we have to follow when we see an angel or we know that there is an angel nearby?

No, that would be rules and regulations, and God is a God of grace. There is not really protocol, but what I like to do is at least wonder why they are there. Some people say, "Oh, you cannot speak to them or you cannot make commands." I think that is the old season. We are moving into a season right now that is very interactive.

I am 58 years old at the time I am writing this and have come through many different seasons with this subject. I came to Jesus the first time in the Jesus People movement of the 70s, fell away and came back in the 80s, then got involved in the prophetic movement in the 90s. So I have been around all this a long time.

I do not have a protocol, but I do ask God. I am not saying it is the only way. It is just probably coming through my filter of being told to do things so many different ways, but I still love asking God. You know, ask Holy Spirit, "God tell me why the angels are here." The first thing you want to do is to determine if it is an angel. No matter what, you will want to test that spirit, and you can say, "I command ..." If there is a protocol, this would be it, "I command right now that you reveal yourself, whether you are the enemy or from the Lord." It takes time to really develop that.

Regarding Robert Henderson's book, *Operating in the Courts of Heaven: Granting God Legal Right to Fulfill His Passion and Answer Our Prayers,* how do the Courts of Heaven relate to favor in the way that Queen Esther found favor with the king? Where does favor come into the process of answering prayer in the Court of Heaven?

Again, when I recommend a book I do not always agree with everything in the book, but that is a great book. I did not quite grasp what he was saying as far that goes, but let me just say this. It matches the template where Queen

Esther went forward, and she got bold. She went forward, got bold, positioned herself and asked for favor. I am not sure if that is what he was getting at, but that is my take on it. He may have meant for us to realize that you are loved and favored like Esther. I do not care if you are male or female. God loves you. Move forward with boldness.

Can we go into the Court of Heaven for other people?

Absolutely. The Court of Heaven is about prayer. This is about going before the Throne boldly.

This is not like a formal process. When we start talking about the Court of Heaven, what we are really trying to get people to understand is that prayer is like this.

You become persistent. Henderson's insight about the battlefield versus the courtroom is very intriguing because we have been out there with the Sword of the Lord cutting the heads off of demons, demanding, battling and wearing ourselves out, yet not seeing a lot of answered prayer.

As far as praying for others, Henderson gives examples of that. In fact, one of his examples is about praying for his son; so that was for someone else. He went into the Court of Heaven. In other words, he did not go into Heaven. He just positioned himself and prayed, and he used the principles God showed him.

Here is how I do it. I use the Bible, and I go in and I pray, "God, this is the promise that You have given my daughter? Your Word says if we bring our requests before You that You are faithful ..."

A speaker at a local church told me that he heard a gavel come down in the Courtroom of Heaven, and the decision was handed down in my favor. But nothing ever happened, and I never saw any fruit from it. What do you think happened?

It could be similar to what can happen in regular court. I have had that happen. I had an encounter where I knew I heard the Lord very clearly regarding a repayment that was due to me. And, yes, a verdict in Heaven was declared. But just like a verdict on Earth, it does not mean that you are going to collect it immediately.

On Earth you have to follow up so you can collect what is legally yours. In prayer, the enemy is going to try to stop you. So you cannot just stop there. You need to keep pleading, going back to see your verdict enforced. The enemy will try to find things against you and try to contest it, just like on Earth, or he may try to take it to an appeals court.

So stay there daily. That is what I do. I stay there daily or weekly, depending on how much you pray. I stay there daily with the promises that I know Heaven has said about me, and I ask that I see them in the natural. Sometimes it takes a year or more to collect. How many times do we see in the legal system that it can take three years until they finally collect? So keep pressing in.

Is there a way you can find out what your destiny is? In other words, can I find out God's perfect will for my life?

Yes there is. It is by noticing and recording clues. God has been leaving clues for you all your life, and they lead to your destiny. To get to the perfect will that the apostle Paul mentions, think of it as a connect-the-dots drawing. Take a look at the dots. Where are you? My connect-the-dots drawing took me to all kinds of things.

Look at what you have been learning. Look at your generations—what they failed at, and also what they are good at. Also, look at what you pretended to be when you were a kid.

Look at the desires of your heart, because Psalm 37:4 says, *"He will give you the desires of your heart."* It does not mean that all your desires are the Lord's, or that they are all part of your high calling. There are clues in there. Pick out those clues and begin to pray for them.

Do not try to jump. Most people try to do the high jump. Even true high jumpers who are called to jump sixteen feet have to start with the lower levels. Where you start will not be where you end up! You know, that perfect will is too high and you are going to work your way up.

How do you go into the Courtrooms of Heaven and ask for justice without accusing another Christian?

Well, I did not say that we cannot ask for justice or go to Court with Christians. I said that too many people are doing it. There is some confusion too about judging. You know, people get all up in arms about it. They are afraid that they might be judging.

I am making observations here because I have been doing this for a long time. Judging would be something negative, so taking something into the Courts of Heaven (like I did with the publisher) when I said, "This is an injustice, Lord." I did it through prayer. It is not like I went into the Courtroom and glibly said, "Hey, Your Honor." I said, "Lord, God, this is an injustice. I have this contract. I have been ripped off. I ask that You move on my behalf. This book was released to change people's lives. It is being held down by the enemy."

Now, that is asking God to render judgment or justice for you. If I were judging, the difference is, judging might also include saying to other people, "Oh, do not use this publishing company. They are terrible. They have been hurting people. They are out of line. They are from the enemy."

So that is the difference. See, that is the negative side of it that comes out of our mouth. We want to be very careful. Judgments often happen on Earth with our disagreements and hurt feelings.

Can I look at my daughter's Book of Life and see her destiny? Can her destiny be changed?

I do not understand why you would want to change someone's destiny. If it means what God wants for her, why in the world would you want it changed? You want to get God's will for them.

It is possible to ask God to see someone's destiny. I do this. I have had various experiences where I am actually there, and I actually see someone's Book of Destiny. I actually just saw one recently, and the Lord showed me how to pray for that person.

You know, you are probably activating. You are seeing into her Book of Destiny already as her parent, but you are not realizing that is what you are doing. You are seeing the calling for her life, but be very careful not to use your own opinion when it comes to that. We can get our soul entangled with our desires for them instead of what God has for them.

How can we pray for our nation in the Courtrooms of Heaven?

You know, the destiny of nations is so important. The biggest thing (and the hardest thing) to get rid of is your opinion. Opinions are not from the Lord. We are now clouded with a political spirit, a political–religious spirit, to be more specific. We are clouded. Jesus never, ever had a political spirit. In fact, those around him and some of His disciples were zealots. They tried to get him to go political. He would not. So that is another downturn that we have had. I am still political and I am a Christian, but I am not out there joining the political–religious spirit. I would rather go into the Courts of Heaven and say, "God, Your will be done over us. Reveal Your will, not my opinion. Reveal what it is that You want to do."

Here is how you do it, and how you can know that you have matured. It does not matter who is in the White House (If you are from the U.S.). Are you praying for them? It does not matter what you think about him, or even what I think about him, he is the President and in an office of honor and we should pray for him. People in the United States who did not understand that Barak Obama was in an office of honor, and refused to pray for him, then they have missed something huge.

In Matthew 23:2–3, Jesus said about the Pharisees: *"The teachers of the law and the Pharisees sit in Moses' seat. So you must be careful to do everything they tell you. But do not do what they do ..."*

This is so important because when you get outside of this understanding of authority, that is cursing and judgment. So ask God to reveal to you how to pray right now because everything is in so much turmoil.

When you are in the Courts of Heaven, are you talking with people? Are you talking with angels?

No. I am praying. When you go into the Court of Heaven, you are positioning yourself to pray. Now, during some experiences, when I am in the Counsel of Heaven, I may go into a Zechariah 3 situation. Sometimes it is my spirit that is there and, yes, sometimes there are other elements, but when you are battling in the Courtroom of Heaven, that is simply prayer. You are praying and trusting God.

ABOUT DOUG

Doug Addison is a prophetic speaker, author and coach. He is known for his *Daily Prophetic Words, Spirit Connection* webcast, podcast and blog. Doug's message of love, hope and having fun reaches people around the world! His powerful, positively funny teaching style and coaching helps open people to discover their destiny and experience God's supernatural love and power. He and his wife Linda live in Los Angeles, California where he is impacting the arts, entertainment and media industries.

DougAddison.com

RESOURCES FROM DOUG ADDISON

Hearing the Voice of God 365

Hearing the Voice of God 365 is an online prophetic activation school that comes to you! Through the twelve modules in this school, you will learn to discern the voice of God every day, grow in your gifts, walk in your identity and discover the destiny God has for you!

Hearing the Voice of God 365 is filled with how–to instruction by Doug, along with exclusive mentoring sessions with prophetic leaders including Lance Wallnau, Lana Vawser, Sandi Krakowski and more. It also provides activation exercises designed to help you learn to hear the voice of God, deepen your relationship with Him and save you time! Learn more at: HearingGod365.com

2017 Prophetic Forecast

In the *2017 Prophetic Forecast*, Doug Addison shares revelation he received regarding the coming revival. Describing the details of several encounters he had with God and messages he received during the Days of Awe (the time period between Rosh Hashanah and Yom Kippur), Doug opens new understanding about what we can expect in 2017 and beyond.

Discovering the Supernatural

Discovering the Supernatural draws from Doug Addison's personal journey and shares stories of his heavenly encounters with God and the angelic realm. In this book, you will get an insider account as Doug addresses the questions he had along the way and answers questions others have asked him as they have learned to hear God and understand the supernatural.

Unlock Your Breakthrough: Self-Coaching Toolkit

The *Unlock Your Breakthrough: Self-Coaching Toolkit* is a result of Doug's over 25 years of coaching himself and others to successfully reach goals. The strategies and tools in this toolkit could be exactly what you need to break through and finally step into your dreams! You will be getting everything you need to go through the process of discovering your life purpose, creating a MAP for your goals, and coaching yourself through any obstacles you face as you go after your destiny. When you join the *Unlocking Your Breakthrough: Self-Coaching Toolkit* you will get the practical strategies and tools you need finally reach your goals.

How to Flip Your Financial Future

This book packs a powerful punch to activate you in practical Kingdom strategies for sowing and reaping, getting out of debt, increasing your income, and even starting or growing your business or ministry, so you can *flip* your financial future ... and flip it good!

God Spoke, Now What?

God is continually speaking to you—sending you messages to help you as you walk through your life journey. Oftentimes, people do not realize when God is speaking to them, and they do not know how to interpret and activate the messages they receive. In his book, *God Spoke, Now What? Activating Your Prophetic Word*, Doug Addison not only shows you how to recognize the messages God is sending you through dreams, life experiences, the media, other people or natural circumstances; he also teaches you how to interpret the messages and activate them so you can see breakthroughs happen in your life.

Write Your Book Now! Online Course

Write Your Book Now! is the all-inclusive online course with everything you need to get your book written and published as quickly as possible—without sacrificing quality. Writing a book used to be a long, painful task, but *Write Your Book Now!* helps you accelerate the writing process so you can have a completed manuscript—in as little as 30 days!

Write a Book Quickly: Unlock Your Creative Spirit

Whether you are just starting out or are an experienced writer, this precise book can help you get to a new level. Tap into your creative nature, learn secrets of writing, publishing tips, writing resources, exercises and more.

Spiritual Identity Theft Exposed

The rise of identity theft in the world today parallels what is happening spiritually to people everywhere. People have been blinded to their true identity and the destiny they were created to live.

Spiritual Identity Theft Exposed contains seven strategies from darkness and seven remedies to change your life forever.

Understand Your Dreams Now: Spiritual Dream Interpretation

Doug Addison's *Understand Your Dreams Now: Spiritual Dream Interpretation,* is drawn from decades of classroom and real–world experiences.

This book contains everything you need to get started or to go to a new level of interpreting dreams. Includes a 300–symbol dream dictionary.

Dream Crash Course Online Training

Understanding dreams does not have to be difficult! Doug Addison is an expert dream interpreter who has interpreted over 25,000 dreams and has trained thousands of dream interpreters worldwide. He has developed a crash course on how to understand your dreams quickly. This is everything you need in one online program. Includes ten online videos, MP3s, study guide, dream journal, symbols dictionary and more!

Prophetic Tattoo and Piercing Interpretation
Online Training

Now you can learn the inside secrets to *Prophetic Tattoo and Piercing Interpretation* from Doug Addison. After years of development, Doug Addison is making this one-of-a-kind online training available to you. Find what you need to get started in this new cutting-edge outreach strategy! This online training includes seven online videos, MP3s, study guide, tattoo reference cards and more.

Visit: DougAddison.store